Foreword by Dr. Bert Herring, MD

JUST
EAT

Planned Eating
Intermittent Fasting Lifestyle

RACHEL
NEKATI

ISBN: 978-99968-0-740-4

Author: Rachel Nekati

Published by: Rachel Nekati

P O Box 602066
Gaborone,
Botswana,
Southern Africa

Email:justeat@rachelnekati.com

www.rachelnekati.com/justeat

Contents

Disclaimer

Just Eat

The information in this book is not a substitute for medical care or advice. Please consult with your physician before you decide to make any changes to your nutrition or exercise routine. If you choose to take action from the information in this book without the consent of your physician, you are accepting full responsibility for your actions and decisions.

Foreword

The world is full of weight-loss promises. Most people who struggle with surplus fat would rather find a solution than commit to a life of acceptance. They may be very frustrated by the awareness that friends with apparently similar diets and activities stay lean without a significant effort. After trying many products, plans and programs, most who want to lose fat develop a high level of skepticism and perhaps an equal portion of despair.

Rachel has been through all of the above: the struggles, the disappointments, the despair, and even some occasional but unsustainable successes. Intermittent Fasting has offered new promise to many struggling to achieve weight loss. It flies in the face of oft-repeated dietary dogma, so questions are a natural reflex. Is it sustainable? Will it work for me? Can I eat foods I like? Will I always be hungry? Will I be grouchy and unpleasant to be around?

In **Just Eat**, Rachel lets you know she has no tolerance for fads or gimmicks. She takes you through her Intermittent Fasting experiences and the pros and cons of the most popular schedule options, then shows her experience is not unique to her body and lifestyle by including the experiences of others: real people with busy schedules, family demands and everyday stresses – people like her; people like you.

Bert Herring, MD

Author of:

> *The Fast-5 Diet and the Fast-5 Lifestyle* **(2005)**
> *AC: The Power of Appetite Correction* **(2015)**

About The Author

Rachel Nekati is a wife and a loving mother to two beautiful children. She graduated from the University of Botswana with a Bachelor of Commerce Degree and has spent fifteen years in the banking industry. She is a Management Training and Business Consultant in her own company, Achievement Enterprises. She facilitates on many accredited soft skills programs, including: Leadership Development, Supervisory and Management Skills, Change Management, Team Building, Customer Service and Emotional Intelligence, to mention but a few. Rachel is also an advanced indoor cycling instructor

Having spent a considerable number of years coaching and mentoring people across the world, she finds joy in sharing knowledge, imparting skills as well as changing people's lives in a positive way.

Intermittent Fasting, learning and understanding the relationship between regular eating, insulin, and fat loss, has been her most enjoyable and enriching discovery.

Rachel is happy to have discovered this simple, sustainable weight-loss plan after having battled with unsustainable weight-loss interventions throughout her life. It is her hope that this lifestyle will change your life, making you slimmer, healthier and happier, just as it has worked for her.

Preface

Just Eat and watch your fat melt away. It seems counter-intuitive in these modern times, when all weight-loss advice is loaded with notions such as:

Don't eat this, don't drink that; weigh this, measure that, count this; wear that.

In the past, if someone had told me instead to "Just eat to a slimmer and healthier you," I would have laughed and carried on blindly counting the calories in a 'tastes just like chocolate' bar that tasted more like cardboard. To my surprise, however, that is precisely what happened to me. For twelve months, I ate anything and everything my heart desired and still saw myself shrinking every week and every month, from size 16 to size 8/10.

There was no counting calories, no measuring portions, no weighing food, no slimming pills, no protein shakes and no excessive exercise.

It is important to understand that once food enters your bloodstream, the pancreas quickly releases the hormone insulin to bring your blood sugar level down. This is known as your blood sugar rush and, after less than two hours, you find yourself reaching for your next snack. Not only does regular eating cause exhaustion, it also causes minimal fat burning. Why so? When you eat, you begin a six- to eight-hour process of digestion, which requires your body to expend a lot of time and energy to break down food molecules that can be absorbed and utilized. This process includes the storage hormone, insulin, which can stay in the bloodstream for six to eight hours post release, preventing fat breakdown.

How then did I successfully, finally get to my now 'goal body' and 'goal size'?

The answer is **Intermittent Fasting**. I knew **when to eat** and **when to stop**.

The day I stopped trying to live by strict 'don't eat this' rules, and started to use a science-driven structure to stay on course, I was no longer chained to overly restrictive diets. I learnt a sustainable way of eating to satiety while naturally balancing my hormonal physical hunger. I ditched the dieting theatrics of aggressive detox, frustrating 'do not eat this' lists, yo-yo dieting-inducing fad diets, juice cleanses, countless weight-loss pills, gallons of tasteless weight-loss teas, and the seemingly endless counting of calories, measuring and weighing.

I came to appreciate that the theory of 'Eating and Stop Eating' is a critical one in determining how much fat you burn as energy. In simple terms, when you eat, you store fat; and when you stop eating, you burn fat. Finally, I understood how to have my cake and eat it too.

My Before And After Pictures

My former top (2017) is now a dress (2018).

Fasting Glossary

IF	Intermittent Fasting
FFA	Free Fatty Acids
16:8, 20:4	The first number is the fasting time and the second number is the eating time.
OMAD	One Meal a Day
ADF	Alternate Day Fasting
WOE	Way of Eating
WOL	Way of Life
Open window	Eating time
Closed window	Fasting time
EF	Extended Fasting
2MAD	Two Meals a Day

AC	Appetite Correction
NSV	Non-Scale Victory
ACV	Apple Cider Vinegar
TOM	Time of the Month
ADF	Alternate Day Fast
CI/CO	Calories In/Calories Out
Clean fast	A non-eating time with no calories, no natural or artificial flavors. This generally consists of water, mineral water, plain sparkling water and coffee or tea with no flavors, sweeteners or creamers.
Keto	Ketogenic

Intermittent Fasting Experiences

"I feel so good and light ever since I started this way of eating, and have high energy levels. The 16:8 eating protocol allows me to have my brunch around 11am and then enjoy dinner with my family in the evening. I don't have cravings anymore and I have no desire to snack during the day. I have comfortably moved from size 14 to 10. My sugar levels and blood pressure are under control. I am happy that my wife introduced me to this way of eating."

W.O.N. from Botswana

"I like being excited to eat. When I was following certain other programs, it felt like I was constantly eating, which meant that I was constantly preparing meals."

A.O. from Canada

"I like the fact that I can eat anything I want and still lose weight. With this lifestyle, I simply fast and feast. I delay not deny. There is no food that is out of bounds. I enjoy giving my body a break to use my stored fat."

K.C. from Botswana

"I like the flexibility of this lifestyle."

A.N. from USA

"I am saving so much time and money. My former dieting habits were too expensive."

K.O. from Slovenia

"Considerably less planning and thinking about food limitations. With IF I only have one meal to plan and look forward to. And yes, this is the cheapest lifestyle."

M.H. from Dublin, Ireland

"It is a lifestyle that is teaching me how to have a more healthy relationship with food. I have learnt to control my desire for food. With IF I feel much better in my body and I am still looking forward to feeling much better."

M.D. from Nigeria

"I love the health benefits. For years I had abdominal pains and diarrhea and no one could tell me what was wrong. I had all kinds of invasive tests. Really invasive. IF has allowed me to rest my GI tract. Now I know what I am sensitive to. IF has changed my life."

J.S. from USA

"IF is easy to follow."

S.L. from Canada

"I am getting results and I can eat food of my choice instead of those boring salads. This is my lifestyle now and I am following it constantly."

K.A.R.M. from Pakistan

Introduction

Overcoming My Thirty Years Of Obesity

Like many people struggling with obesity, while growing up I turned to food for comfort, and I cannot remember a time when I considered myself slim. I was not fond of eating large meals, preferring to snack constantly. I always liked to have something to munch on, whether that be fruits, sweets, a protein bar or even chocolate. Regular small meals and treats throughout the day was my way of life. To me, food was never simply fuel, nor was it just for hunger. It was a means of keeping myself occupied. Following the passing of my parents in my teenage years, eating became even more of an emotional crutch. I remember keeping my bedtime snacks of chocolates and crisps under my pillow. This proved to be the start of my obese life.

Due to my size, school sporting activities became a challenge. I remember the discomfort I experienced during the dreadful school athletics seasons at school. These were the times when, during the high school year, the house team runners were selected. To determine who the fast runners were, everyone in school was expected to race. Typically, the teachers always targeted the slow runners, the ones who were expected to finish last in the race. They would join the race right at the back, wielding a long, black twine whip, and lashed out at the slow runners for their suspected 'laziness', which was hardly ever the case. Thus, the ones trailing would usually get the most lashings. Not only was this an uncomfortable experience, it made me hate sports even more and is the reason why I decided not to participate in any form of physical activity during high school, with the exception of table tennis, which I found bearable as there was no running involved.

University days were no easier. I preferred to study late at night as it was always calm and quiet with minimal or no disruptions. Regular exams and tests meant lots of studying, and my approach to staying awake involved regular snacking. These snacks could be anything from biscuits, sweets and chocolates to fizzy drinks and, my personal favorite, bread with jam. However, this did not make my weight management any easier since it meant that my insulin levels were always high, causing me to store fat.

My early twenties saw additional responsibilities: marriage, a growing career and parenting. Life was happening, with all that came with it. By then, my life demands and challenges resulted in a significant increase of loops on my emotional roller coaster. The great and challenging times made me further cling to the only thing that made me feel comfortable, and that was putting some delicious food in my mouth! I always found comfort in the taste and feel of food, and snacking was my easy escape from the demands and stress of my increasingly busy and demanding life.

With all these weight gains, yo-yo dieting became my way of life for the next thirty years. I remember carrying a small cooler box everywhere, every day, containing all kinds of healthy snacks and smoothies that I would nibble on at regular intervals. Though some yo-yo diet interventions resulted in significant weight loss, the joy gained from such losses was very short-lived. Though I reasonably managed the weight gained during two pregnancies through strict, drastic, weight-loss methods, the weight kept on creeping back. Eventually, I realised the problem was that such weight-loss interventions were unsustainable and that I was unable to easily continue with them as a way of life. I came to appreciate that, for any weight loss to be sustainable, I had to do something that I could more easily make a permanent part of my lifestyle. It does not matter how effective something might seem at first, what matters most is whether you can do it for the rest of your life. That is where my challenge lay.

The main issue was that I had always believed that I should eat every two to three hours to maintain my metabolism and avoid getting into a 'starvation mode'.

It's only now, at the age of 45 that I have come to acknowledge and accept the fact that the reason why I had been struggling with my weight was basically that my regular eating had made me insensitive to insulin, which had been on overdrive for the past thirty years, making weight loss impossible. My body never had the opportunity to convert any of my stored fat into energy as I was always in a fed state.

I'll describe in more detail what I mean by 'insulin resistance' further on in this book, but here follows a brief description.

Insulin Resistance

Insulin resistance is the name given to the state when cells of the body do not respond properly to the hormone insulin. This resistance is closely associated with obesity. The role of insulin in the body is to allow cells to take in glucose in order to be used as fuel or, alternatively, stored as fat. If a person is insulin resistant, it means that glucose is more likely to build up in the blood and this can lead to high blood sugar levels. When the body becomes resistant to insulin, it tries to cope by producing more insulin. People with insulin resistance are often producing too much insulin compared with healthy people. Because I was insulin resistant, I had developed some signs and symptoms which, at that time, could not be understood or explained. I was having unexplained weight gains irrespective of my healthy active lifestyle and was also diagnosed with high blood pressure in 2013. Moreover, I was experiencing some inflammation in my knees and toes to the extent that I went to the doctor to check if I had arthritis or gout. Although the test results all came back negative, the pain and inflammation were still there and, unfortunately, I could not get any convincing explanation for why I had them.

For many years, scientists and nutritionists have

preached that weight loss simply comes down to an equation of 'calories in versus calories out'. While this principle can be true under normal circumstances, there are a number of increasingly common hormonal shifts that can alter the seemingly basic weight-loss equation. Insulin resistance is normally a clinical condition that precedes type-2 diabetes. A person with insulin resistance will struggle to lose weight via a traditional 'calories in versus calories out' approach, as had been my case. My body was simply not burning fuel the way it should. I remember sometime in November 2016, sitting in my doctor's office weighing 94kg (207lbs) doing my routine medical tests. Concerned, I asked my doctor why I was struggling to lose weight even though I was eating healthily, exercising regularly and even tracking my calories. The response I got was that maybe it had to do with my genes.

It was only after discovering and researching Intermittent Fasting (IF) and insulin that I discovered that, irrespective of my healthy eating and intense exercise routine, my body was simply not burning enough fuel to lose weight. IF has been my greatest breakthrough.

Chapter 1

Emotions And Their
Effects On Eating Habits

I have discovered that my previous regular snacking lifestyle was, to a large extent, driven by my emotions. Sometimes, the strongest food cravings hit when you're at your weakest point emotionally – when facing difficulties, feeling stressed or even bored. Hence, like the old me, you may turn to food for comfort, consciously or unconsciously. You may not be aware of it, but it's important to watch your patterns of behavior when you are experiencing a roller coaster of feelings. Expressions such as "I wish I could have a chocolate", "I feel like having a glass of wine" or "I could finish a tub of ice cream" could simply indicate that the driving force for those cravings is basically caused by that emotion which you are trying to suppress as opposed to the physical hunger. This kind of eating is called emotional eating. There is nothing wrong with wanting to soothe an inner wound, except when it is taken too far. That compulsion to soothe oneself could end up messing with your life path in ways you would not have wanted. Food has a tremendously powerful impact on our lives and, as such, it can be used to nourish, strengthen and heal. However, it can also be used to soothe and numb to an excessive degree. The pleasure of food can work as a powerful soother as much as any drug and that can lead to overeating, obesity and other health problems. Obesity often comes with its own additional self-negativity, over and above the original wound that one was trying to soothe with regular snacking or excessive food.

It is not hard to be afflicted by an emotional eating disorder because almost everyone knows that food is something that's easy to get and, somehow, people think that comfort eating will not do harm to their bodies - after all, we all need food to live. Depression, guilt, anxiety, chronic frustration and stress are some of the things that one could experience when one is in the throes of emotional eating. One may also be afflicted with diseases or ailments such as diabetes, high blood pressure, depression, anxiety, menstrual and digestive problems. The hassles of daily life can trigger negative emotions that lead to emotional eating. Some of the triggers are:

- The loss of a loved one
- Family conflicts
- Relationship challenges
- Stress at work and home
- Fatigue
- Money issues
- Deteriorating health
- Anxiety
- Boredom
- School pressure
- Peer pressure

Although some people eat less in the face of strong emotions, if you're in emotional distress you might turn to impulsive or binge eating, quickly consuming whatever is convenient, sometimes even if it is without enjoyment. A person might find the act of eating very useful in easing the discomfort. In fact, your emotions can become so tied to your eating habits that you automatically reach for a treat whenever you're angry or stressed without thinking about what you're doing. Food, in this instance, is basically being used to serve as a distraction.

Think of a scenario when you're worried about an upcoming event or constantly worrying over a certain conflict, it is very easy to focus on eating comfort food instead of dealing with the stressful situation.

Whatever emotions drive an individual to overeat or constantly snack, the end result is often the same. The emotions usually return, and you likely then bear the additional burden of guilt about setting back your physical and emotional health. This approach normally results in an unhealthy cycle, thus your emotions will make you overeat and then you feel guilty about how you look and feel and you overeat again. The cycle goes on.

Dealing With Emotions Through Intermittent Fasting

My discovery of IF has helped me deal with my emotions. Dealing with emotions is an important part of IF that a lot of people do not discuss. In fact, I found this to be the real purpose of fasting, over and above other health benefits including weight loss. Dealing with emotions helps one to discover, understand, control and express emotions in a positive way. This is what is meant by 'emotional intelligence'. To be emotionally intelligent, a person needs to be self-aware, to understand the emotion they are feeling at any point in time. This requires some reflection, introspection and active listening to your body without any distractions. It is important to accept what the emotion is, as well as to appreciate why you are feeling that emotion, so take time to listen to what that emotion is trying to communicate to you. It is counterproductive to ignore, blame or accuse yourself for feeling that way. Simply acknowledging that this is the way you feel is very important.

It is only after accepting the emotion you are feeling that you can consider how to make yourself feel better and, to do that, you must master the skill of managing your behavior in response to such strong emotions.

Intermittent Fasting And Self-Management

IF means deliberately cycling between periods of eating and not eating (feasting and fasting). The eating time is referred to as the 'open window' whilst the not eating time is referred to as the 'closed window'. My experience is that, during my closed window, I allow myself to listen to my emotions and the break from food gives my body time to focus on many other things. I often experience clarity of mind which allows me to put things into perspective. It will be during that time that I self-assess and also assess my interactions with people. At times, I make a note of my emotions to understand what they are trying to tell me. A short break from eating helps me learn not to turn to food when I have an emotional issue and has benefited me greatly. I am able to face and deal with whatever emotion I experience at any particular time without turning to comfort snacking or eating.

Something most of us can relate to is going through an interpersonal conflict; you might be feeling sadness, grief, stress or anger. However, rather than dealing with emotions, often we try to bury them and turn to food instead; we are 'burying those molecules in our bodies'. This is a person's 'emotional baggage' as the saying goes. Sometimes one can literally identify a person's emotional baggage in the form of excess weight or an illness. However, when you take a break from eating, that is, close your food window, you have no choice but to face and deal with whatever emotion comes to you. It is not possible to stop dealing with your emotions when comfort food is not an option. Instead, a process of internal cleansing begins. My experience with IF has been that, when I am fasting I feel calmer and more capable of putting things into perspective. This is such a humbling experience and a beautiful time of release. The reality is that when you push through these emotions, you will get the real rewards. It is like digging for hidden treasure and for me, it feels like I am truly digging deeper to the essence of who I am. With IF come the additional benefits of cleaning your colon and regenerating your physical body. Fasting also assists with stripping away emotional traumas and deeply held things that have been within us potentially our whole life.

Usually, without even realizing it, from a very young age we tend to build up layers – or a shield – around us. For example, think of the first time you went for a job interview, and you were all excited and happy until someone said to you, "I don't think you are good enough for the job" without necessarily telling you why. That will be the time that you subconsciously begin to put up layers around your heart to protect yourself. This is a natural instinct. Now you are finding it difficult to get rid of these layers. Subconsciously you are operating on a level that is still afraid to express who you truly are. Sometimes it could simply be based on a difficult experience that might have happened when you were young. Even if that experience might currently not even be relevant anymore, it could still be affecting you on that deeper level. Fasting will allow you to go through a process where you can begin to strip away these old patterns of behavior.

The Difference Between Emotional Hunger And Physical Hunger

We are all normally driven to eat by hunger, a physiological impulse hard-wired into our brains and bodies. Hunger is regulated in the brain by the hypothalamus, which signals when the body is satisfied and when it needs more food to reach that state. Emotional hunger can be powerful so it's easy to mistake it for physical hunger. However, there are clues you can look for to help you tell physical and emotional hunger apart. Fasting can be a powerful tool to recalibrate your relationship with eating habits and perceived hunger. It may take some practice but once you reconnect with the feeling of true hunger, you can follow your body's lead and eat whenever the feeling strikes.

Emotional Versus Physical Hunger

Emotional Hunger Comes On Suddenly

It hits you in an instant and feels overwhelming and urgent. Physical hunger, on the other hand, comes on more gradually. The urge to eat doesn't feel as dire nor does it demand instant satisfaction unless you haven't eaten for a very long time.

Emotional Hunger Craves Specific Comfort Foods

When you're physically hungry, almost anything sounds good, even healthy stuff like vegetables and fruits. But emotional hunger craves junk food or sugary snacks that provide an instant rush. You feel like you *need* cheesecake, sweets, chocolate or pizza, etc., and nothing else will do.

Emotional Hunger Often Leads To Mindless Eating

Before you know it, you've eaten a whole bag of chips or an entire tub of ice cream without really paying attention or fully enjoying it. When you're eating in response to physical hunger, you're typically more aware of what you're doing.

Emotional Hunger Isn't Satisfied Once You're Full

You keep wanting more and more, often eating until you're uncomfortably stuffed. Physical hunger, on the other hand, doesn't need to be stuffed. You feel satisfied when your stomach is full.

Emotional Hunger Isn't Located In The Stomach

Rather than a growling belly or a pang in your stomach, when you are emotionally hungry, you feel your hunger as a craving which you can't get out of your head. You're focused on specific textures, tastes and smells, such as chocolate, bread, sweets, fizzy drinks, cake, pizza, ice cream and alcohol. Does this sound familiar?

Emotional Hunger Often Leads To Regret, Guilt Or Shame

When you eat to satisfy physical hunger, you're unlikely to feel guilty or ashamed because you're simply giving your body what it needs. If you feel guilty after you eat, it's more likely because you know deep down that you're eating for the wrong reasons.

Physical And Emotional Hunger Summary

Physical Hunger	Versus	Emotional Hunger
• Can be satisfied with any type of food such as fruits and vegetables		• Causes specific cravings for, among others, sweets, pizza, chocolate and ice cream
• Comes on gradually and it can be postponed		• It comes on suddenly and feels urgent
• Causes satisfaction not guilt		• Leaves one feeling guilty and cross with oneself
• You can stop eating once full		• You overeat until you feel uncomfortably full

Identifying Your Emotional Eating Triggers

IF can help you to identify situations, places or feelings which make you reach for comfort food. Most emotional eating is linked to unpleasant feelings, but it can also be triggered by positive emotions, such as rewarding yourself for achieving a goal or celebrating a holiday or happy event. As mentioned before, some of the common causes of emotional eating could include:

Stress

Stress normally makes a person hungry. It is not just in your mind. When stress is chronic, as it so often is in our chaotic, fast-paced world, your body gets too highly strung. This can easily lead to high levels of the stress hormone, cortisol, which in turn triggers cravings for salty, sweet and fried foods that give you a burst of energy and pleasure. The more uncontrolled stress in one's life, the more likely you are to turn to food for emotional relief.

Stuffing Emotions

Eating can be a way to temporarily silence or 'stuff down' uncomfortable emotions, including anger, fear, sadness, anxiety, loneliness, resentment and shame. While you're numbing yourself with food, you can temporarily think that you are successfully avoiding the difficult emotions you'd rather not feel. This is a temporary relief which will normally later turn to guilt because you have overeaten.

Boredom Or Feelings Of Emptiness

Sometimes one eats just to keep oneself busy or just to fill a void in one's life. At times when you feel unfulfilled or empty, it is easy to use food to occupy your mouth and your time. In the moment, it fills you up and distracts you from underlying feelings of purposelessness and dissatisfaction with your life.

Childhood Habits

Think back to your childhood memories of food. It might be that your parents rewarded good behavior with ice cream, took you out for pizza when you got good grades, baked you a cake for any positive celebration or sometimes served you sweets when you were feeling sad. It is possible to carry over these habits into adulthood. Sometimes, your way of eating may be driven by nostalgia for those cherished memories of barbeque steaks and sweetcorn by the poolside with your dad whilst your mum is preparing those mouthwatering salads and desserts.

Social Influences

Family, Friends and Food – the three Fs which go together so well. Getting together with the people you love for a meal is a great way to connect, but it can also lead to unnecessary overeating. It is easy to overindulge simply because the food is there or because everyone else is eating. You may also overeat in social situations out of nervousness or perhaps your family or circle of friends encourages you to overeat, and it's easier to go along with the group. I remember times when I would choose not to eat or delay my meals. All that I could hear my family and friends say was, "Rachel, you are afraid of food."

Other Ways To Manage Your Feelings

If you do not know how to manage your emotions in a way that does not involve food, you will not be able to control your eating habits for very long. Diets so often fail because they offer logical nutritional advice which only works if you are able to control your eating habits. It does not work when emotions hijack the process, demanding an immediate relief with food or another emotion suppressant. In order to stop emotional eating, you have to find other ways to fulfill or satisfy yourself emotionally. It is not enough to understand the cycle of emotional eating or even to understand its triggers, although that's a huge first step. You need alternatives to food that you can turn to for emotional fulfillment.

Alternatives To Emotional Eating

1. If you're depressed or lonely, call someone who always makes you feel better, play with your pet, look at your photo albums or remember cherished moments.
2. If you're anxious, expend your nervous energy by dancing to your favorite song, squeezing a stress ball, taking a brisk walk or going to the gym.
3. If you're exhausted, treat yourself to a hot cup of tea, have a spa day or light some scented candles and take a long bath.
4. If you're bored, read a good book, watch a comedy show, explore the outdoors or turn to an activity you enjoy such as sewing, rearranging your house, playing the guitar, listening to your favorite music, doing a bit of scrapbooking, playing your favorite song or dancing.

Emotional eating tends to be automatic and virtually mindless. Before you even realize what you're doing, you've reached for a tub of ice cream and polished off half of it. But, if you can take a moment to pause and reflect when you're experiencing a craving, you give yourself the opportunity to make a different decision. Always ask yourself if you are still hungry after you have put off eating for five minutes or maybe even just one minute. Don't tell yourself you *can't* give in to the craving; remember, the forbidden is extremely tempting. Just tell yourself to wait. Delaying might do you good as opposed to depriving yourself entirely. While you're waiting, check in with yourself. How are you feeling? What's going on emotionally? Even if you end up eating, you'll have a better understanding of why you did it. This can help you set yourself up for a different response next time.

Intermittent Fasting Boosts Neuronal Autophagy And Mind Clarity

Contrary to popular concerns, fasting has potentially incredible benefits for various brain functions, perhaps the greatest being the activation of autophagy, a cellular cleansing process. Recently, one of the pioneers of research into autophagy, Yoshinori Ohsumi, was awarded the 2016 Nobel Prize in Physiology or Medicine in growing recognition of this pathway of diseases. IF is said to induce neuronal autophagy. Autophagy, or 'self-eating', is the process by which cells recycle waste material, regulate wasteful processes and repair themselves. Brain health is highly dependent on neuronal autophagy. Fasting also has a known antiseizure effect. In mammals, mental activity increases when hungry and decreases with satiation. We all have experienced 'food coma'. Think of a large Sunday family lunch and all kinds of desserts and drinks. After that large meal, do you feel mentally sharp? Or do you feel dull as a concrete block? How about the opposite? Think about a time when you were really hungry. Were you tired and slothful? Probably not. Your senses were probably hyper alert and your brain was probably as sharp as a needle. The idea that food makes you concentrate better is entirely incorrect. There is a large survival advantage to animals that are cognitively sharp as well as physically agile during a time of food scarcity. When we say you are hungry for something, hungry for power, hungry for attention, does it mean that you are slothful and dull? No, it means that you are hyper vigilant and energetic. So it is reasonable to say, fasting and hunger clearly activate us towards our goals. We tend to worry that fasting will dull our senses, but in fact, it has the opposite, energizing effect.

IF can assist one to practise self-awareness and self-management. The practice of staying away from food during set times gives one the opportunity to understand every emotion they feel at any point in time and helps a person assess why they feel the way they feel. This process of introspection always results in giving a person inner calm, peace of mind and allows one to control and successfully manage their emotions.

Intermittent Fasting And Self-Awareness

1. Know And Understand Yourself

Sometimes, you have to think about things and reflect on your life. Think about who you are and where you are right now. Is this what you want for your life? Is this the kind of life that you pictured for yourself long ago, or is there something else you want? By getting to know yourself again, you will realize some things about yourself and get to know if there are things that you want to do.

2. Develop An Emotional Journal

Learn how to deal with things or with the problems that you encounter. Here's what you can do. Take a sheet of paper and make a list of all the things that have been bothering you recently. From your smallest worries and woes, to the big things that have been plaguing you for a long time, write them all down and try to see what could be done. By listing these things, you can have a better sense of clarity and you will also learn how to start planning to make your life better. Don't worry too much. Worrying only wastes time, plus it will also make you more stressed. Stress does nothing good for your mind and your body, so stop worrying too much.

3. Start A Hobby

Do something that is totally unrelated to your job. Do arts and crafts, if you feel like it. Read books, write, listen to music, upload your own song covers to YouTube if you want to, make music videos, write poems, do some gardening, maybe even do some Pilates. The point is, you have to find something to do with your time that's not related to eating.

4. Scheduled, Inflexible 'Me' Time

Learn how to love yourself again. How hard can it be? If you do not learn to love yourself, then surely life is hard. If you cannot deal with yourself, how can you expect others to deal with you? Spend some time with yourself. Go on a holiday. Visit a relative. Learn how to enjoy time alone. You have to remember that you are a beautiful, unique person and that you have all these strengths (even if you do not seem to see them all the time) that make you a great person.

5. Create Like-Minded Support Structures

Keep in touch with your family and friends. Stay connected to those who have been with you for a long time and whom you know you can trust. These could also be people you share the same interests and hobbies with. Sometimes, we all need to feel that someone is there for us and that's why it's important that you keep the lines of communication open between you and the people in your life. I found my support groups, Let The Body Go and Just Eat Intermittent Fasting Lifestyle, very supportive, encouraging and motivating.

6. Develop Realistic Goals

Visualize. Do you know that researchers agree that once someone visualizes what they want for the future, then there's a high percentage that what they have been visualizing will come true? That's true. Put up a corkboard in your room and pin pictures or letters/notes that say something about what you want to achieve, where you want to go or what kind of person you want to be.

7. Visualize How You Will Look After Achieving Your Goal

Have faith and talk about your goal in present terms. See yourself as someone who has already achieved their goal. Sometimes, a person's life will be in better balance when this person knows that they can do it. This could also be realized by the belief in a higher power. By having something to believe in, you will feel that you are not alone and that life has so much in store for you. Remember to always consider any setbacks as temporary.

Chapter 2

My Yo-Yo Diets Roller Coaster

While making an effort to manage my weight for better health reasons, I got myself trapped on a diet roller coaster. Although none of them gave me sustainable results, giving up was never an option. Looking at my book collections, among many other books, I have an entire library of all kinds of diet books – dating as far back as 1995. It is not an understatement when I say I have tried as many diets as one could ever think of. At all times my weight fluctuated between 105kg (231lbs) and 79kg (174lbs). With my height at 165cm (5'4"), according to my BMI, I was either medically very obese, obese or in the overweight category most of the time.

My Thirty Years Yo-Yo Diets Bank And Weight-Loss Interventions

My desperate attempts to keep my weight within acceptable ranges both for health reasons and to achieve my goal size led me to the darkest life of diets and frustration. That was the most depressing and uncertain lifestyle one could ever experience. Not only is it expensive today, it is emotionally and physically draining since nothing is good enough. Even if something works today, you cannot expect the same outcome in the future. Your happiness becomes a function of the number you see on the scales so, if the number goes down, you celebrate but, if the number goes up, your happiness flies out of the window. This desperation leads one to seek out anything and everything carrying the phrase, 'quick weight loss'.

I would like share with you my past weight-loss interventions which, I must say, did result in short-term weight loss and translated to exciting moments at that time. Those short-lived moments saw me dropping a size or two and even changing my wardrobe accordingly, but unfortunately that wardrobe often became obsolete when the weight returned.

Below are some of the diets I have tried this far:

I.   Fat Free

On this diet, I could only eat fat-free food and food products. Any full-cream or low-cream food was forbidden. I was made to believe that fats are bad and anything with more than 3g fat per 100g was not allowed.

2. Low Fat

Unlike the fat-free diet, this diet allowed slightly higher amounts of fat as compared to the fat-free diet plan. Only low-fat foods were allowed in the house. Low-fat margarine; low-fat ice cream; low-fat peach slices; low-fat chocolate; low-fat milk; low-fat yoghurt; low-fat custard; low-fat juice; low-fat protein shakes; low-fat protein bars; low-fat cheese and low-fat crisps. This became my family's way of life. Though my family were supportive of these forever-changing food choices I was making, they expressed their concern with regard to me shopping for low-fat products as opposed to 'normal' products, since low fat was all that I bought from grocery stores. And so, to keep everyone happy, I resorted to buying both my low-fat products and my family's 'normal' products. You can imagine how much I was spending on groceries. And worse still, my weight did not change because I was snacking on these low-fat products throughout the day, thus keeping my insulin levels too high.

3. Slimming And Fat-Burning Pills

Just the thought of pills makes me sick these days. For almost all my life, I have been trying all kinds of fat-loss and weight-loss pills. I naively believed that popping a pill would melt away fat and make it disappear forever while blithely continuing to eat my three meals per day plus snacks.

Think of any weight-loss pill brand. I have tried them all. Some of the brands were only available internationally, and that meant importing them regardless of the cost. All that was important to me at that time was to lose weight. It is sad to think how desperate a person can be when they want to lose weight. Not only does a person become gullible to faddy marketing, one also quickly forgets that the previous attempts did not work. We do not easily learn from past mistakes, but rather find ourselves addicted to the diets and weight-loss gimmicks

4. Carbohydrate Blockers

With 'carb blockers', as they were known, I was made to believe that I could eat as many carbohydrates as I desired as long as I had taken this pill prior to my eating. These pills promised to block carbs from being digested, apparently allowing me to eat carbs without worrying about piling on unwanted calories. That basically was a license to indulge as much as I wanted at any time. Unfortunately, this initiative made me gain more weight than before.

5. Fat Blockers

Fat blockers promised to ensure that all the fat calories I consumed were not successfully absorbed by the body, caused by some special ingredient that attaches itself to the fat. However, just like the carb blockers, it didn't work.

6. Slim Body Wraps

This was supposed to be my fat-melting breakthrough. The infomercial claimed that if I rubbed the fat-burning cream on my targeted areas and then wore their product (a belt) twice a day for ten to twenty minutes per session, then my body fat would melt away. I thought I had finally found something that would solve my fat issues once and for all. All I can say is no fat or centimeters were lost and I was very sweaty after each session.

7. Liquid Diet

As the name suggests, this liquid diet meant I would be getting all, or at least most, of my calories from drinks; no chewing was allowed. Everything that I wanted to digest should only be in a liquid form. This liquid diet limited me to fruit and vegetable juices, or soups that replaced all of my meals, taken three or four times a day. And though I did experience slight weight reduction, I soon hit a plateau after losing just a few kilograms.

8. Food Combination Eating Plan

The fat-burning food combination plan allowed me to eat anything I wanted, as long as I followed the rules. In general, I could eat the following food combinations:

- A protein with non-starchy vegetables (example: stir-fried chicken with green beans)
- A starch with any vegetables or with legumes (example: rice with kidney beans or black beans)
- A starch with fats

The plan advocated that these combinations don't interfere with the digestion or metabolism of proteins, starch or fats. After eating what's allowed, I would need to wait a few hours for my food to digest before I could eat any food that was not in the combination. Well, I did lose some weight with this lifestyle but the weight all came back within a short period of time after I reverted to eating 'normally', thinking that I had succeeded in losing weight.

9. Eating For My Blood Type

I remember, after discovering this plan, I immediately made an appointment with my family doctor to check and confirm my blood type as well as that of my entire family. (When I look back at how supportive my family have always been, I feel so grateful for their support throughout my interesting weight-loss journey.)

This diet concept, simply put, recommends that everyone should follow an optimal diet according to whether their blood type is A, B, AB or O. The plan advocates that certain foods are good for your blood type, and that others are dangerous. Eat foods from the latter category, and you may experience a variety of health issues, ranging from inflammation and bloating to a slower metabolism and even diseases such as cancer (or so the book says). I don't remember having any success with this diet at all.

10. Raw Food Diet

Advocates of raw food diets believe that the typical diet of processed foods, animal products, pasteurized foods and chemical additives contributes to diseases such as diabetes and high-blood pressure. Another theory surrounding this raw food diet is that when we cook our food, we break down the food's enzymes and lose many of the food's nutritional benefits. A raw food diet is usually strictly vegetarian, although some in the raw food movement allow unpasteurized dairy products, raw meat, raw eggs and sushi. I remember following this diet for a very short time and then quitting since I love my meat and bread. I found this diet to be too restrictive and did not fit in with my lifestyle. We are a family that loves a variety of meats so this diet could not work for me.

11. Protein Diet

Proponents of this diet claim that I could lose weight while eating as much protein and fat as I wanted, as long as I avoided foods high in carbohydrates. Initially, I lost some weight on this diet when I followed it to the last detail. However, any time I introduced even the slightest quantity of carbohydrates, the weight would all come back. My love for bread did not make this way of eating enjoyable or sustainable.

12. Computerized Slimming

In 2001, I enrolled in a slimming clinic that offered this service. Within six months I lost 30kg (66lbs) and moved three sizes down. I hit my lowest weight ever, down from 105kg (231lbs) to 75kg (165lbs), and went from size UK 18 to size UK 12. Electrical muscle stimulation, also known as neuromuscular electrical stimulation or electro-muscular stimulation (EMS), is the elicitation of muscle contraction using electrical impulses. It is full body training using electrical stimulation. In this method, the muscles are stimulated so that the workout is much more efficient. EMS was said to cause strengthening, toning and firming of muscles, resulting in a super-effective workout in a short time span, thus effectively creating an overall weight loss. Over and above the EMS sessions, I also followed a specific eating plan which eliminated most carbohydrates. A maximum of 20g of carbohydrates was all that was allowed per day. With this eating plan, counting carbohydrates in each and every food item was the order of the day. I should acknowledge though that this machine became my most preferred weight-loss method or 'sweet spot' since I managed to lose 30kg (66lbs) in a few months. I was so motivated that I turned this computerized slimming clinic into a business. I thought to myself if it worked this well on me then I should also help others who are struggling with weight issues. I went through the computerized slimming consultant training, sourced the machines and opened my own slimming clinic. The slimming clinic helped a number of people to lose weight and some were able to keep the weight off longer, provided they kept their daily carbohydrate intake between 20g and 40g. So, on the face of it, this method does provide some pleasing results. One can clearly say the success of this weight loss was mainly because it was a combination of electro-muscular stimulation therapy with a very low carbohydrate diet. Unfortunately, like other diets, keeping to a maximum of 20g to 40g carbohydrates for the rest of your life is not sustainable. This way of life proved to be a challenge to maintain, especially for someone like me who likes to eat from all the food groups.

13. Two Protein Shakes A Day

Here I go again on another liquid diet. Protein shakes are believed to promote muscle growth and repair after exercise and could be a quick meal replacement when one is on the go. Drinking two protein shakes instead of full meals daily assisted me with weight loss, but it proved not to be a long-term weight management solution. These shakes made it easy to cut calories but, at some point, when I returned to whole foods the weight simply piled back on. Even when I felt that this was my best ticket to weight loss, I had to carefully choose the shakes I consumed and consider whether they were the best options for my health goals. On this diet plan, all I needed to do was replace just one or two meals (usually breakfast and lunch) with protein shakes, and then I could eat a healthy protein-rich meal with vegetables and salad for dinner. I was allowed some healthy snacks on this plan. Protein bars, peanuts, biltong, cheese and fruits were always my favorite snacks during the course of the day. This resulted in some weight loss. However, it proved not to be sustainable because, more often than not, I preferred to eat real food than have my meals in a liquid form.

14. Low-Carb Diet

A low-carb diet means that you eat fewer carbohydrates and a higher proportion of fat. On this plan, I was to only eat when I was hungry, until I was satisfied. It sounded simple since I did not need to count calories or weigh my food. For a change, I could forget about industrially produced low-fat products since there was no reason to fear natural fats. Fat was said to be my friend, I simply had to strictly minimize my intake of sugar and starches. Though I lost a considerable amount of weight, I felt deprived since I mostly preferred a balanced sustainable way to live with no restriction on what I should eat.

15. Calories In/Calories Out Lifestyle

Numbers, numbers and numbers. Counting and weighing was my order of the day, I downloaded an app which assisted me with the tracking of everything that was going into my mouth. I remember one day my husband saying to me that the way I was obsessing about these numbers, one day it would turn into a disorder. This eating plan is based on the understanding that when you eat more calories than you burn, you gain weight. Tracking calories and keeping up a calorie deficit can result in a significant weight loss. How many calories you need depends on factors like gender, age, weight and activity level. If you are trying to lose weight, you will need to create a calorie deficit by eating less than your body burns off. However, even though I calculated my daily allowance to lose weight and included a lot of vigorous exercises in my lifestyle, I still did not lose weight. I did experience a slight reduction in my fat percentage but, when it came to weight loss, it did not work for me. In my life I have had a number of personal trainers and have also enrolled in a number of boot camps and still my weight did not move.

I remember one particular boot camp, doing our exercises in the outside car parking lot on very cold early winter mornings at 5am. As cold and early as it was, I was so determined to do whatever it took to shake off this weight. Though the coach was very good and experienced at what he did, the fact that we were encouraged to have a pre-workout snack and post-workout protein shake followed by small meals every three hours did no good managing my insulin. Even though I was burning a lot of calories, the fact that my insulin was always high, it made fat burning difficult. There were times I exercised twelve hours a week, burning on average 800–1,000 calories per hour to ensure that at all times I could remain in a calorific deficit state. Though these workouts improved my body physique, weight loss was still a challenge.

16. Cabbage Diet

Supposedly, following this diet for seven days can lead to weight loss of up to 10lbs (4.5kg). For seven days you eat almost nothing but homemade cabbage soup. Each day, you can also have one or two other foods, such as skimmed milk, fruit or vegetables.

Many sources claim the diet works not by acting as a starvation diet, but rather because cabbage is such a low-calorie food that your body ends up burning more calories digesting it than the cabbage itself contains. Therefore, the more soup you eat, the more weight you lose. Though I slightly lost the weight, it all came back the moment I started a balanced meal. Like other diets I had tried before, this also proved to be unsustainable and I could not live on cabbage soup for days.

17. Onion Diet

The onion soup diet is similar to the more famous cabbage soup diet, and involves eating onion-based soup as a staple food for a full week. The diet calls for participants to eat the homemade, onion-based soup every day as their main meal item. On Day one, fruit is also allowed, except for bananas. On Day two, vegetables are permitted. Day three allows fruits and vegetables, and Day four also allows skimmed milk. Followers may eat tomatoes and some meat or fish on Day five, beef and vegetables on Day six and brown rice, vegetables and fruit juice on the last day. As the soup is so low in calories, it is claimed to encourage weight loss. However, the soup neglects to satisfy all nutritional needs, and the weight loss was never permanent.

18. Egg Diet

This is a low-carbohydrate, low-calorie, but protein-heavy diet. It is designed to help aid in weight loss. Like its name suggests, it emphasizes the consumption of eggs as a main source of protein. Foods high in carbohydrates and natural sugars, like most fruits and all breads, pastas, and rice are eliminated from the diet, which typically lasts fourteen days. You only eat breakfast, lunch, and dinner. There are no snacks, aside from water or other zero-calorie drinks. Even though I love eggs, I found this eating plan not sustainable since I had to eliminate other food groups.

19. Clean Eating

It was December 2016 and I was on holiday. As usual, I was reading one of my favorite fitness books when I came across a story about a lady who had lost a significant amount of weight through clean eating. I took some time to research on this eating plan and I found it to make a lot of sense. The flexibility of 80/20 made me want to try this lifestyle which I did in January 2017. This lifestyle advocates eating 80 per cent clean or non-processed food with a 20 per cent flexibility of eating whatever I wanted. The principle of clean eating is consuming food the way nature delivers it, or as close to it as possible. Non-processed food means: beef, chicken, lamb, pork, fruits and vegetables. The other 20 per cent would come from bread, pasta, rice, yoghurt, cheese, chocolate and wine. I did not find this way of eating restrictive and I enjoyed it. However, the fact that this plan advocated three meals and two to three small snacks simply meant that my insulin was constantly high. I should admit though that I enjoyed this way of eating and within twelve weeks I lost 5kg/11lbs. I felt great and my skin greatly improved.

Unfortunately, as usual, I hit a plateau after losing my initial 5kg (11lbs). It was during this time when I decided to share with my fitness pal colleagues that I had hit a plateau. One lady recommended that I should try IF. I knew nothing about this but I'm so grateful to that lady for saying those words.

Chapter 3

Trying To Use Exercise To Manage My Weight Through Calorie Deficit

I believed so much in the 'calories in versus calories out' idea that, not only did I count calories, I always ensured that I did activities which would result in significant calorie expenditure. This included jogging 10 to 15km per day, skipping rope (I could do 2,000 jumps a day with ease), and two to three hours in the gym. All this was to ensure that my weight-loss formula could be correct, thus: CI *(Calories In)* – CO *(Calories Out)* = *Negative (Deficit)*

Before discovering the impact of insulin on my weight loss, I believed wholeheartedly in the principle of maintaining deficit calories. My belief was that even though I kept snacking every two to three hours, as long as I maintained a calorie deficit my weight should come down. Unfortunately, despite burning thousands of calories per day, this routine did not lead to sustained weight loss.

According to a certain scientific calculator, I was given these daily calorie allowances:

To maintain my weight	2,480 calories
To lose weight	1,984 calories
To lose weight fast	1,488 calories

These figures were not a problem to achieve and I ensured I used a calorie tracker to monitor all my meals and activities. Talk about exercising! I exhausted myself doing vigorous exercise but once I realized my weight-loss results were very minimal, I thought I would never be able to shed excess weight. My daily calorie expenditure and maintenance of a deficit did not prove to be very helpful to my situation. This proved the widely known belief that weight loss is mainly 20 per cent exercise and 80 per cent food. My experience on the other hand has been, for effective good health and weight loss, 20 per cent exercise and 80 per cent IF. This is based on my experience, a 'study of one'.

Before discovering the IF lifestyle, I exercised as much as I could to maximize calorie expenditure. Some of my friends even thought I was an exercise addict but this didn't bother me as I was focused on my personal goal. At times I was exercising twice a day, burning between 1,500 and 2,000 calories and, when combined with eating within my calorie allowance, achieving my weight-loss goals seemed very achievable.

Even though I had never been a binge eater, I was a three-meals-a-day-and-three-snacks sort of person. Exercising and burning calories was my priority and I ensured that my calorie allowance was always 'on a deficit'.

My eating habits, however, did not prove to be very helpful. I would have a pre-workout snack, a post-workout protein shake, a high-protein breakfast, a high-protein lunch, a mid-afternoon snack or protein bar, dinner and a piece of fruit for dessert. My meals and snacks were mostly healthy and due to the fact that I combined these with a vigorous exercise plan, I expected this way of life to solve my weight-loss issues. Despite all of this, it just did not work. My weight reduced slightly but I soon plateaued between 98kg (216lbs) and 92kg (202lbs).

So, in 2015, I decided to take my exercising to another level. I became a certified advanced indoor cycling Instructor. My husband decided to do the accreditation with me since we both have a love for the thrill of indoor cycling. I remember the first day of my accreditation program in South Africa. Looking around at the group of participants, it seemed like I was the only oversized person in the group. Every other future instructor looked to be well toned and in good shape, with not much visible excess fat.

During our indoor cycling training, the facilitator emphasized the importance of looking the part and living by example as fitness instructors. That didn't really bother me since I was confident that becoming an indoor cycling instructor would be a permanent solution to all my recurring weight-loss issues. Immediately after my accreditation I started instructing three intense classes per week at two different gyms, which strengthened both my determination and my commitment to this highly active life.

Despite this active lifestyle and clean eating, I was still stuck on a three-meals-and-three-snacks-a-day regime (which as I mentioned earlier did not prove to be helpful to my own particular situation). I came to realize that I could not solely rely on an active lifestyle with six meals to solve my weight issues.

I enjoyed and still enjoy my active life. However, it became evident that regardless of how much I exercised, as long as I was eating that many meals, nothing could happen, even though I was also on a clean eating plan. High insulin was hindering my fat-burning process. I am sure you are wondering how much weight I lost after becoming an indoor cycling instructor. Well, my weight still plateaued at 92kg (202lbs). Due to my height (165cm/5'4"), my BMI still placed me in the obese category. CI/CO with six (healthy) meals spread through the day did not work for me. Something had to change.

Chapter 4

Unlocking The Secret To My Weight Loss Through Intermittent Fasting

After being on a weight-loss roller coaster for thirty years, I decided to dive headlong into a twelve-month self-experimentation with IF. I had tried pretty much every other weight-loss method without success, so I thought I had nothing to lose, except perhaps some weight. I'll really get into the details in this chapter but the thing that really differentiates IF from all the other methods is what it can teach you about yourself and how your emotional state dictates what food you put into your body. I am now able to differentiate true or physical hunger from emotional hunger. I also discovered that for my body to burn off the stored fat I have to **JUST EAT** and then **STOP EATING** when I am satisfied. Feast and Fast.

To elaborate, I could eat whatever I wanted but then

make sure I stopped eating when I was full, and then not have anything else to eat for anything between sixteen and twenty-four-hours, depending on how hungry I felt. A few weeks after adopting the IF lifestyle, I could not stop being amazed at the rate at which my body fat was melting away. But how did it happen?

1. After eating a meal, my blood sugar level rises and insulin is produced to counter this rise. This blood sugar is the energy or calories my body uses to function properly. When I stop eating for a long time, my blood sugar and insulin levels get lower, as well as the amount of glycogen being stored. When this happens, my body has no choice but to start burning fat for energy. Body fat is just the accumulation of all the excess energy a person produces every time a person eats more than their body requires. However, the body is forced to access the stored fat only when the blood sugar is low. The regularly raised insulin which was the case with my previous lifestyle, with three meals and regular snacking, hindered my body from utilizing the stored fat.

2. When I stop eating for some time – when fasting – my body responds to this by releasing more adrenaline which in turn causes me to have more energy, be more alert and focused. As my body releases adrenaline, it induces the burning of fat,

mainly the stubborn fat on the belly, thighs and hips in order to give me the needed energy after my insulin level has lowered. The body does this because this is how the body was designed. It simply stores fat for periods of no food and then releases the energy when it is needed.

How Did My Eating Patterns Change?

I eat my meals within a smaller time frame. IF is not a diet but rather a pattern of eating. I restrict my eating times each day to between one and eight hours, depending on how I feel and as my schedule allows. When there is a social event, I adjust my eating times to accommodate it. I do not operate on hard, rigid rules, I live and enjoy myself. When I started this way of eating (WOE), I would finish eating my dinner (known as 'closing the window') at 8pm and then have a brunch at noon the following day. That basically would give my body sixteen hours of no food after my last meal. (This period is referred to as 'fasted state' or 'closed window'). After having my meal at noon, my next meal would be dinner at 7pm. These two meals would be normal meals with food from all food groups without depriving me of anything. (Yay!)

The science behind this is that, during the fasting state, stored fat is constantly broken down by the body and is converted into energy. This is a situation that is ideal for weight loss and long-term weight management as the body's overall capabilities for fat burning are hugely maximized. During the first four weeks of practicing this lifestyle, I would usually eat my first meal any time between noon and 1pm and stop eating at any time between 8pm and 9pm until the following day. I did not snack or take any calorific fluids except water, plain tea or coffee until between noon and 1pm the following day. When it was time to eat, I ate anything I desired without eliminating any food groups. I simply ate a normal lunch followed by dinner in the evening and thereafter, I would close the eating window any time between 8pm and 9pm. So dinner time was fun since I simply enjoyed whatever my family was enjoying in the evenings. There was no longer that fussy mum who obsesses about measuring, weighing and even avoiding certain foods.

After four weeks, I realized that I was getting less and less hungry around 1pm though I had not had breakfast. So gradually I started feeling hunger pangs around 5pm and therefore I decided to push my first meal forward to 5pm. I think my body was now fat adapted, I was becoming more efficient in utilizing my stored body fat for energy. The fact that I had more energy stored as fat, meant my body was mastering the art of diving directly to these stored reserves for energy.

When I started this lifestyle, my body fat was 49 per cent versus my target of 20 per cent. One can say I really had a 'bank of stored fat' to withdraw from and that is why I was feeling less hungry during the morning and day. Having shorter eating times seemed to be what my body preferred since I always had an overwhelming amount of energy throughout the day and I even did all my workouts in a fasted state with great success. The important thing is not to force yourself into eating just because it is time to eat or the window is open. Personally I don't force myself to eat at 5pm. Rather, I simply listen to my body and start eating (open my window) when my body tells me to. I would usually open my window with a healthy snack, my favorite being cherry tomatoes and olives, or roasted peanuts, plain yogurt with a mixed berry smoothie or sometimes just a piece of fruit. From experience, I realized that if I opened my window with a highly processed food item, my body became bloated and at times I would even get stomach cramps.

I learnt to listen to what my body wants and my body wants to have just one meal a day. I always make sure my one meal is very special and nutritious and most of all, consists of three courses.

I look forward to my three-course dinner every day.

There is nothing forbidden or out of boundaries. I mostly prefer nutritious meals and some treats. With regard to weekends and special occasions, I simply extend my open window from a four-hour eating window to anything between six and eight hours. It is this flexible approach that I appreciate. This lifestyle works, it's easy, it's flexible and there is no cost.

This is what my typical day would be like:

5pm   Open window with a non-processed snack

7pm   Have dinner. I would eat anything my family would be eating on that day. Sometimes I would even have a starter, my favorite being soup and homemade bread. A dessert or sometimes a glass of wine would make my meal complete.

9pm   Close the window after dinner

I am not usually rigid about my eating times, I simply listen to my body. As long as my minimum fasting hours of twenty has been achieved I simply decide whether I should eat immediately or wait for another few hours which will then coincide with dinner time. Say for example my twenty-hour fasting time ends at 5pm. If I am not hungry at that time, I don't force myself to eat, rather I will wait until the time when I will feel hungry, and **Just Eat**. In a nutshell, with this way of eating, you are either fasting for twenty hours, or eating for the next four hours over your feeding window. After that four-hour feeding period, you would repeat the fasting for the next twenty hours. Generally, most people place their four-hour feeding window at the end of the day, as it's more convenient for family dinners and after-work social sessions. However, modifications can be made based on the individual and scheduling preferences.

My Weekly Eating Protocol

Monday: 22:2 (Intermittent Fasting) IF

The first number is the fasting duration and the second number is the feasting or eating duration. Therefore, 22:2 IF means fasting for twenty-two hours after the previous day's meal and then having my dinner within two hours of the end of the twenty-two-hour period. I would stop eating on Sunday at 9:30pm and would have my next meal on Monday, between 7:30pm and 9.30pm, after my workout.

Tuesday, Wednesday and Friday: 20:4 IF

This means fasting for twenty hours after the previous day's meal and then having my dinner within four hours of the end of that twenty-hour period. I would stop eating at 9pm and my next meal would be the next day between 5pm and 9pm.

Thursday: 23:1 IF

You can probably work out what this means but, for clarity, it means fasting for twenty-three hours after the previous day's meal and then having my dinner within one hour of the end of that twenty-three-hour period. So if my previous meal was on Wednesday at 9pm, my next meal would be on Thursday at 8pm, usually after my workout.

Saturday, Sunday And Special Occasions

On these days I usually relax my time to allow social events. Therefore, I have a longer open window. Managing my time this way allows me to accommodate social occasions without necessarily depriving myself. On 'special days', I simply aim for a closed window lasting a minimum of fourteen to sixteen hours after my last meal and this will remain flexible, opening my window as and when I want to. If there is nothing that requires me to open my window, I usually simply choose to shorten my closed window.

Ever since making these changes and having become fat adapted, my appetite has also been corrected. My body communicates well to say when it is satisfied and I listen. I allow myself to eat when I feel physically hungry. It is important to bear in mind that this lifestyle is meant to be enjoyable rather than to be viewed as self-denial or maybe punishment. These regular flexible variations of time keep my body guessing and to some extent minimize the possibility of plateauing. This is what I like about this lifestyle; it's flexible, fun, refreshing and very easy to do.

I cannot describe how happy I am that IF has greatly simplified my life. I no longer think or obsess about snacks and food all day, neither do I find it necessary to carry a snacks cooler bag around. All I carry is water.

In an interview with *Vanity Fair*, President Obama described an interesting strategy he uses to make his life simpler. During the interview he said, "You will see that I wear only grey or blue suits. I'm trying to pare down decisions. I don't want to make decisions about what to wear because I have too many other decisions to make." What the President was referring to is a concept called 'decision fatigue' and it can drastically impact your ability to make decisions throughout the day. As for me, simplifying my meal frequency through IF provides me with the same benefit. Eliminating breakfast and sometimes lunch and not making decisions about food until 1pm or 5pm each day has allowed me to focus on more important decisions to do with all the other facets of my life.

This way of eating has reduced my decision fatigue and has also increased my willpower that I have for the rest of the day. I usually find myself with more energy to put towards doing what is important to me. I believe that one of the best ways of finding happiness and success in life is by stripping away the unnecessary things and focusing only on what is needed. With IF, I enjoy increased strength, eliminated body inflammation, reduced body fat and good health, while spending less time on eating each day. If a person can get great results by making life simpler, by only eating once or sometimes twice per day, why would one prefer to make life more complex by eating three, four, five or six times per day? You can naturally and organically sculpt the body, your real body that is hidden under all that excess weight and fat you are carrying around.

IF is not a quick weight-loss diet but rather a natural healthy lifestyle choice. You don't have to starve yourself because feeling hungry is proof that your metabolism is working and if you fast for sixteen or twenty hours after you have eaten what you want during your eight- or four-hour window, you really can't call that starving.

I have learnt that to ease into this lifestyle, you don't have to radically adjust your life or emotionally swing wildly from terror to dread whenever it is time to eat. Simply work with your body, listen to your body and if you feel physically hungry, **Just Eat**. This is not a life sentence. It is the most liberating way of working with your body. And whenever I remembered the numbers I used to see on my bathroom scale and how that used to make me feel, I felt motivated to make this way of eating my permanent lifestyle. I took some time to think about what is right for my health instead of jumping on the latest diet bandwagon. The concept of fasting is surely nothing new. Scientific studies on its benefits have been around since the 1940s, and it is found all over the world and surely goes all the way back to the beginning of human existence when food was not available twenty-four hours a day like it is now. The theory that we need to eat many small meals all day long and never allow ourselves to feel hungry, which is commonly taught as the method to maintain a high metabolism, is being debunked, whilst the benefits of increasing the duration between meals have become too numerous to ignore.

One of the overarching concepts is that as the body has to spend less time and resources on the high-energy task of digestion, it has a greater capacity to focus on activities that benefit us in many other ways. These activities include cleaning the body of toxins, repairing and rebuilding muscle tissue, and putting the body in an ideal state to burn body fat and lose weight. All these activities have a significant potential to increase our body's ability to avoid diseases as well as improve the body's natural detoxification process known as autophagy.

Autophagy

Cleaning and detoxifying is something our bodies do all the time and it happens twenty-four hours a day. The millions of cellular processes that happen every day put pressure on individual cells, particularly the mitochondria. Ideally, the body identifies these worn-out cells and replaces them. This process is called autophagy. While this process is automatic and ongoing, poor diet as well as overeating can significantly slow down this detoxification process.

On October 2016, the Nobel Assembly at Karolinska Institute awarded the Nobel Prize in Physiology or Medicine to Yoshinori Ohsumi for his discoveries of the mechanism for autophagy. [1]

The Nobel Prize winner discovered and elucidated on the mechanism underlying autophagy, a fundamental process of degrading and recycling cellular components. It has been said the word autophagy originates from the Greek words *auto*, meaning self and *phagein* meaning to eat. The word literally means to eat oneself, or 'self-eating'. This is the body's mechanism for getting rid of all the broken down, old cell machinery (proteins and cell membranes) when there is no longer enough energy to sustain it. It is a regulated, orderly process to degrade and recycle old cellular components. This concept is said to have emerged during the 1960s, when researchers first observed that the cell could easily destroy its own contents by enclosing membranes, forming sac-like vesicles that are transported to a recycling compartment, called the lysosome, for degradation. I recommend that you read this research in detail in order to have a better understanding of this process. However, I can briefly sum up the process of autophagy by saying, when the body is digesting incoming food or when the body is in a fed state, cellular custodial duties are normally slowed down.

Therefore it is important to give the body time to focus solely on cellular repair and optimal cleansing through fasting. Interestingly, some researchers have indicated the benefits of fasting on neuron-centric diseases like Alzheimer's. As autophagy is increased during a fasting state, the run-down mitochondria and other cellular molecules are eliminated from the neurons. We can clearly see then the connection between the increased detoxification abilities while fasting and another benefit is a decreased aging process. Fasting has been proven to be a significant cleansing process.

Generally, the IF lifestyle is to a large extent about empowering your metabolism to burn off your unused energy which is stored as fat whilst allowing your body to use what has been stored for a while. Later on, you can then eat sensibly without sacrificing what you want to eat. **Just Eat.**

Chapter 5

What Is Intermittent Fasting?

IF is a term for an eating pattern that switches between periods of eating and total abstinence from food, or cyclical patterns of feasting and fasting. Thankfully, it does not prescribe **what** you should eat but rather **when** you should eat. The science behind IF is not complicated. It simply means that during the period of not eating, stored fat is constantly broken down by your body and gets converted into energy. This is a situation that is ideal for weight loss and long-term weight management as your body's overall capabilities for fat burning are hugely maximized. For that reason, IF is not a diet in the conventional sense. It is best regarded as an eating pattern or plan which involves the practice of willingly eliminating or limiting your intake of foods and beverages during specific times of the day or days of the week. It is all about making a conscious decision to defer or skip certain meals on purpose. Alternating periods of eating and not eating can help build your immune system, trim down your fat and keep you healthy.

Fed And Fasted State

When you eat a meal, your body spends a few hours processing that food, burning what it can from what you have just consumed. Because it has all of this readily available, easy-to-burn energy, your body will choose to use that as energy rather than the fat you have stored. This is especially true if you have just consumed a high-carbohydrate meal, as your body prefers to burn sugar as energy before any other source. During the fasted state, your body does not have a recently consumed meal to use as energy, so it is more likely to pull from the fat stored in your body as it's the only energy source readily available and that results in the body burning fat. Without a ready supply of glucose and glycogen to pull from, your body is forced to adapt and pull from the only source of energy available to it – the fat stored in your cells.

How Does This Work?

Insulin and glucagon are hormones that help regulate the blood sugar (glucose) levels in your body. Glucose, which comes from the food you eat, moves through your bloodstream to help fuel your body. Insulin and glucagon work together to balance your blood sugar levels, keeping them in the range that your body requires.

During the digestion process, foods that contain carbohydrates are converted into glucose. Most of this glucose is sent into the bloodstream, causing a rise in blood glucose levels. This increase in blood glucose signals your pancreas to produce insulin. The insulin then tells cells throughout your body to take in glucose from your bloodstream. As the glucose moves into your cells, your glucose levels go down since some cells are using the glucose for energy. Other cells, such as those in your liver and muscles, will store any excess glucose as a substance called glycogen which your body will use in between meals as energy.

About four to six hours after your meal, the glucose level in your blood decreases, triggering your pancreas to produce glucagon. This hormone signals your liver and muscles to change the stored glycogen back into glucose. The cells then release the glucose into your bloodstream so your other cells can use it for energy. Glucagon plays an active role in allowing the body to regulate the utilization of glucose and fat. As discussed, glucagon is released in response to low blood glucose levels and times when the body needs additional glucose, such as in response to vigorous exercise. When glucagon is released it stimulates the liver to break down glycogen to be released into the blood as glucose, breaking down stored fat (triglycerides) into fatty acids for use as fuel by the cells. The role of insulin, on the other hand, is to allow the cells of the body to take glucose to be used as fuel or stored as body fat.

The more sensitive your body is to insulin, the more likely it is you'll be able to use the food you consume efficiently, which can assist with weight loss and muscle creation. IF can significantly increase our body's sensitivity to insulin which is an ideal situation especially for a person who is insulin resistant.

Insulin Sensitivity

Insulin sensitivity describes how sensitive the body is to the effects of insulin. Someone who is said to be insulin sensitive will require smaller amounts of insulin to lower blood glucose than someone who is insulin resistant. Low insulin sensitivity can lead to a variety of health problems since the body will be under pressure to try and compensate for having a low sensitivity to insulin by producing more insulin. However, high levels of insulin, known as hyperinsulinemia, can cause damage to blood vessels, high blood pressure, heart disease, heart failure, obesity, osteoporosis and even cancer.

Insulin Resistance

Insulin resistance is when the body cells do not respond to the hormone insulin and this can lead to pre diabetes and type-2 diabetes. Insulin resistance has been the cause of my own inability to lose weight, regardless of clean eating and exercise. It made me remain in the obesity category throughout my life. IF has greatly helped me to teach my body to use the food I consume more efficiently, and my body has learnt to burn fat as fuel when I deprive it of new calories. For many different physiological reasons, IF helps to promote weight loss and muscle building due to the Human Growth Home (HGH) which naturally increases during fasting periods.

The Facts Of Intermittent Fasting

As far back as the 1930s, scientists have been exploring the benefits of IF through skipping meals. During that time, one American scientist found that significantly reducing calories helped mice live longer, healthier lives. The finding suggested that limiting food intake may reduce the risk of many common diseases and some experienced that fasting increased their body's responsiveness to insulin which regulates blood sugar and helps control hunger.

The five most common methods of IF try to take advantage of each of these benefits. However, different methods will yield better results for different people. Considering the fact people have a unique genetic makeup, metabolism and gut health as well as different food tolerances, it will not be ideal to compare someone else's results with yours.

"If you're going to force yourself to follow a certain method, it's not going to work," says trainer and fitness expert Nia Shanks. "Choose a method that makes your life easier," she says. Otherwise, it's not sustainable and the benefits of your fasting may be short-lived.

So what is the first step in getting started? Each method has its own guidelines for how long to fast and some methods also prescribe what to eat during the 'feeding' (or 'open window') phase.

I have shared my preferred fasting protocol which best suits my lifestyle in my twelve- month journal at the end of this book. I however explained the five most popular methods and the basics of how they work so that you can pick and choose what works for you. I found it useful to be flexible and rotate my fasting protocols depending on how I feel.

Keep in mind, IF is not for everyone. Those with health conditions of any kind should check with their doctor before changing their usual routine. Note that personal goals and lifestyle are key factors to consider when choosing a fasting method and what you plan to eat during your open window time. When making a decision on what to eat, consider how humans have been thriving off organic real food for thousands of years. An eating plan consisting of more of the non-processed food can liberate a person from obesity and other chronic illnesses like diabetes and heart disease. This will assist in making a person healthy and typically lean. Remember to always nourish your body. *Eat to live, don't live to eat.*

My secrets to a sustainable regular eating plan are:

- ## Keep It Simple

  Listen to what your body is saying and work with your body. With the IF lifestyle you will find yourself no longer obsessing about food and you will eat less frequently, allowing your body to focus on other important tasks. Eating more natural foods, such as meat, fish, a variety of leafy green vegetables, legumes, fruits and healthy fats, will fill you up faster and you will see yourself eat less, which will in turn help you to shed fat without much effort. Although I enjoy my treats of processed food, I strive to ensure that it makes up no more than 20 per cent of my overall eating plan. When I started this lifestyle, weight loss was my main goal. Therefore, I kept my meals mostly simple with more non-processed food types. I preferred dishes which did not have a long list of extra ingredients and additional flavorings, ensuring that meals with a long list of ingredients were treats to be had only in moderation.

- ## Just Eat Until Satisfied

Many people think that eating less food is always ideal when it comes to weight loss. Not only does this deprive your body of the nutrients it needs to function optimally, it can also lead to bingeing, which is never good for anyone and will lead to stress. With IF, you eat until you are satisfied and then you stop eating until later. Losing weight should never be about starving yourself. When it's time to eat, **Just Eat** and indulge yourself until you are satisfied. Though some might argue that calories do count when it comes to eating, when it comes to weight loss, undereating is just as problematic as overeating.

- ### Stay Active

Stay active throughout the day. Even though staying active is not mandatory with this lifestyle, it is the best way to generally live. Exercise alone is not enough to reverse the harmful effects of too much sitting. Be moderately active throughout the day. For instance, use the stairs instead of an elevator, park your car a few meters from the shops to allow you to walk to and from the shop, walk your dogs, clean your house, do some gardening or wash the car. All these tasks and more contribute to staying active. This habit of staying active will accelerate your fat loss while following this easy lifestyle. Get active throughout the day as this is great for cardiovascular well-being and promotes a well-rounded regimen.

- ### Manage Your Holistic Life Balance

Try to understand your daily life stress trigger because life balance is very important to achieving an optimal lifestyle. You need to assess and address the following parts of your life: psychological, social, physical, financial, emotional and spiritual. Otherwise, if they are not adequately addressed, they can counteract your efforts. An elevated amount of stress triggers cortisol which in turn could trigger insulin and thus compromise the fat-burning state which you are trying to reach through IF. Cortisol can also play tricks with your appetite. It therefore makes sense that we tend to feel like putting something in the mouth when under stress. Sleep time should also not be overlooked. Ensure you get enough sleep – six to eight hours of sleep is the normal recommendation. Sleep is key to a sound and healthy lifestyle. It helps the body regenerate and recover after each day – we need adequate sleep, not too little and not too much. Poorly regulated sleep patterns can lead to catastrophic manifestation on our physical bodies hence the need for proper management.

- Establish Good Support Structures

There is nothing as difficult as trying to do things on your own and this also can be the case when it comes to weight loss. The weight-loss road can be frustrating, lonely, dark and confusing. I was fortunate to have a solid support team and cheerleaders during this process of 'study of one'. I have walked this narrow path with supportive people who have shown solidarity by adopting this way of eating for themselves. (You will have the opportunity to read their testimonials in the success stories chapter at the end of this book.) With the support from my team, I was able to handle stress, keep on track and also hold myself accountable. This made my journey enjoyable and we all have developed into a team of coaches and mentors.

Although other people are able to lose weight whilst eating anything they want during their open window, you will do well to remember that we are all different and you always need to ensure that you nourish your body and pay attention to the nutritional value of the food that you eat.

As I have previously indicated, among many other reasons why I love IF, one is that I did not have to religiously count calories, neither did I have to restrict carbohydrates to lose weight. I mainly ensured that my meals were made up of healthy natural food that helped me to stay full longer. Not having to count every morsel of food that passes through my lips is one other reason why I decided to make this way of eating a permanent lifestyle. For once in my life I did not have to eliminate any food I love, but rather I enjoyed all my favorite foods. I enjoy meals from various food groups: red meat, eggs, grains, legumes, dairy, fish, olives, olive oil, nuts and a variety of fruits and vegetables. I feel much relieved that I no longer have to starve myself with banal powdered shakes, bland meal replacements and protein bars.

Having said that, nourishing your body should motivate you to follow the 80/20 rule when it comes to your eating pattern. 80 per cent natural food and 20 per cent processed food. This is not a rocket science formula, but rather an ideal split to consider when in doubt of how much of each food to consider eating.

You simply cannot live on treats only. *You should eat to live, not live to eat.* Personally, I have realized through my journey that my body positively responds if I eat real natural food 80 per cent of the time especially for my first meal after fasting. If I decide to open my window with anything processed, my body reacts with stomach cramps and discomfort. When I say natural foods, I mainly refer to food that is not processed such as fruit, vegetables, meat, chicken etc.

Benefits of Intermittent Fasting

1. Weight Loss

Instead of running on fuel from the food you just ate, fasting allows your body to tap into reserves – fat, which accumulates in the body to be burned whenever the food supply grows scarce. This results in a steady weight loss that can be a huge benefit. Since fasting is often incorporated as a lifestyle change instead of a temporary fix, this type of diet is much more sustainable than many other 'crash diets'. In fact, many studies, including [2], support the practice as a valuable, reliable tool for weight loss and weight maintenance. According to the article, they found that intermittent restriction was as effective as continuous restriction for improving weight loss, insulin sensitivity and other health benefits.

2. Improves Tolerance Of Glucose

For diabetics, fasting can be a fantastic way to normalize glucose and even improve glucose variability. Anyone looking for a natural way to increase insulin sensitivity should attempt an intermittent fast, as the effects of fasting can make a huge difference to how your body processes glucose. As discussed, insulin resistance is the result of an accumulation of glucose in tissues. As the body burns through stored fuel in the form of body fat, that excess accumulation becomes smaller and smaller, allowing the cells in your muscles and liver to grow increasingly responsive to insulin, which is great news for anyone looking to be less dependent on medication to assist these processes.

3. Boosts Metabolism

Part of the reason IF helps practitioners lose weight is because the restriction of food followed by regular eating can help stimulate the metabolism. The shorter fasts promoted by IF have proven to increase metabolism by up to 14 per cent, according to the *Journal of the Academy of Nutrition and Dietetics* [3]. Comparing this finding with my personal experimentation, I can attest to this increased energy toward the end of the fasting times.

As an indoor cycling instructor, most of my classes are in the evening and I do all my workouts in a fasted state. Not only do I feel fine and not hungry at all during these workouts, my energy levels will normally be very high. I always experience an overwhelming energy towards the end of my fasting times. IF can be said to be a more effective tool than long-term calorie restriction, which can often wreak havoc on the body's metabolism. Extreme low calorie restriction often goes hand in hand with muscle loss. Since muscle tissue is what suffers through extreme calorie restriction, having less muscle leads to a drop in your body's ability to metabolize food. IF, though, keeps your metabolism running smoothly by helping you maintain your muscle tissue as much as possible.

4. Appetite Correction [4]

Appetite Correction (AC), a revolutionary new focus in weight loss based on ten years of user experience with Dr Bert Herring, is a ground-breaking guide to daily IF. In Dr Bert's book, *AC: The Power of Appetite Correction*, AC means getting your body's appetite center working again. Not only do you lose excess fat, you lose it without being hungry and once you have lost the weight, it stays off if you maintain the flexible, low effort AC lifestyle. He states that, when your appetite center is working well, you do not want to eat more than you need. He continues to state that a working appetite center means:

- You recover control over food
- No calorie counting is required – your appetite center does the counting automatically
- No food is off limits. Even wine, beer and candy are allowed
- It saves money and time
- You work with your body instead of fighting it

I encourage you to read his book for more details since it is very informative.

5. Longevity

Research from University of Chicago scientists revealed that IF can "delay the development of the disorders that lead to death", meaning that regular practitioners can enjoy a longer, healthier life than people who regularly eat three meals a day or follow a traditional restricted-calorie diet.

A theory on this, according to the head of the National Institute on Aging's neuroscience laboratory, Mark Mattson [5] is that the mild stress IF puts on the body provides a constant threat, increasing the body's powerful cellular defenses against potential molecular damage. IF stimulates the body to maintain and repair tissues and has anti-aging benefits, keeping every organ and cell functioning effectively and efficiently.

6. Helps With The Ability To Understand Physical Hunger

It is important to learn how to accurately understand the signals your body gives you, and IF is a great way to understand the cycle of hunger. It is common to confuse emotional desires with hunger, but fasting will give you the opportunity to experience real hunger pains in the stomach, and even withdrawal and detox symptoms associated with our usual consumption of processed foods. You will also develop a deeper appreciation of food. If you have ever eaten after a period of true hunger, you will know what eating is supposed to feel like. Each bite tastes more delicious than the last, and you will experience a sensation of deep contentment and pleasure. It is absolutely worth the hunger you endured to get there.

7. Helps To Establish Routine

Unless you are following a random fast type of diet, having strict eating times followed by periods of fasting can help your body develop a solid routine. You will be able to recognize your own hunger cycles, you will sleep more regularly and soundly and you will start scheduling appointments during convenient hours. Though it might seem to be difficult to establish this routine at first, establishing an eating and not eating time around your lifestyle is important. Fasting should not make you feel like you are deprived: rather, it should be flexible, practical and enjoyable. You will realize that once you have developed a workable plan, you will soon start to see all the ways a set routine can benefit your life and your health.

8. Stimulates Brain Function

In a study [6] discussed at a meeting of the Society for Neuroscience in 2015, it was revealed that IF offers "enormous implications for brain health". According to the study, which was undertaken on both humans and animals, fasting stimulates the brain in a number of different ways: promoting the growth of neurons, aiding in recovery following a stroke or other brain injury and enhancing memory performance. Not only does IF help decrease the risk of developing neurodegenerative diseases like Parkinson's or Alzheimer's, evidence shows it may actually even improve both cognitive function and quality of life for people living with those conditions.

9. Boosts Immune System

According to the research [7], immune system defects are at the center of aging and a range of diseases. In another study, according to scientists at the University of Southern California, fasting has the power to "regenerate the entire immune system" by boosting the production of new white blood cells, which is how your body fights off infection. Fasting in cycles, like most practitioners of IF will do on a daily or weekly basis, enables your body to purge the damaged, old or inefficient parts of the immune system and replace them with newly generated immune system cells. Studies showed that a seventy-two-hour fast was possibly enough to help protect cancer patients from the harmful and toxic effects of chemotherapy treatments which generally cause significant damage to the patient's immune system. Further clinical trials are needed, but many researchers are confident that IF could be incredibly helpful for immune-compromised individuals and the elderly.

10. Rejuvenates Skin

Acne sufferers know one of the best ways to control bothersome skin conditions is through diet, eating only unprocessed foods and limiting the consumption of dairy products. It is no surprise that regular IF can offer impressive benefits that can be seen on a practitioner's radiant face. I personally did not find the need to continue using certain facial products since my skin improved significantly and it is no longer as oily as it used to be before I adopted the IF lifestyle.

Many skin conditions are caused by food sensitivities, which can lead to inflammatory conditions and acne. If you want to consider using IF to reduce skin sensitivities caused by food allergies, after a fast, introduce foods one at a time and note any changes to your skin to accurately pinpoint which foods should be avoided. IF also has a positive effect on hair and nails, helping them grow healthy and strong. Not only will you feel good after incorporating IF into your lifestyle, you will look great too.

11. Promotes Inner Calmness

A lifestyle that includes IF normally leads to a deepened sense of inner calm. My experience with IF is that I normally feel calm and at peace during my fasts. Studies have even proven that fasting can help regulate mood by reducing levels of anxiety and stress. In fact, fasting is recommended as a natural treatment for a variety of emotional problems and abuses. IF usually helps a person feel more connected to nature and the environment around and you will benefit from having a clear mind and a positive outlook. According to the survey [8], this way of eating has attracted attention due to its evident effect on the neuroendocrine system and mood condition. Clinicians found that prolonged fasting reduces negative emotions in patients suffering from eating disorders. It also relieved negative moods like tension, anger and confusion.

12. Reduces Oxidative Stress

Oxidative stress is caused by an imbalance in the body's production of reactive oxygen and its anti-oxidative defenses, and may lead to chronic diseases and cancers. Unstable molecules, known as free radicals, can react with important molecules like DNA and protein, damaging these molecules and creating an imbalance. The weight reduction brought on by regular IF can lead to a reduction in the body's level of oxidative stress and helps to prevent the development of these unpleasant conditions. A greater antioxidant capability is a huge benefit that comes with IF and one that should not be overlooked by anyone seeking to pursue improved health and well-being. According to the survey done [9], eating less can extend your life span and helps to prevent age-related diseases.

13. Improves Heart Function

A lower body fat percentage has wide-reaching benefits through the entire body, but possibly none more important than in cardiac function. Consistently, studies such as [10], have found IF has facilitated weight loss preventing the progression of type-2 diabetes and improving cardiovascular health. According to the report, extensive evidence suggests that imposing fasting periods upon experimental laboratory animals increased longevity, improved health and reduced diseases, including diverse morbidities of cancer, neurological disorders and disorder of the circadian rhythm. The report further says that IF in animal models produces some cardiovascular benefits such as improving blood pressure and heart rate, as well as circulating cholesterol and triglycerides. Some studies have further indicated that IF can lead to a reduction in cholesterol levels – particularly triglycerides, which the body uses to create energy. Having less body fat also takes some strain off the kidneys, lowering blood pressure and increasing the body's production of growth hormones. Combined, these benefits can mean a significant improvement in heart function.

14. Could Help To Prevent Cancer

IF's impressive ability to stimulate growth hormone production is also important for possibly reducing a practitioner's risk of developing a number of types of cancer. Regular eating triggers the body into producing more and more new cells which can inadvertently speed up the growth of certain cancer cells. Fasting, however, gives your body a bit of a rest from this activity, and lessens the possibility of new cells becoming cancerous. In addition, studies have indicated that when combined with chemotherapy, IF can help the immune system in attacking breast cancer and skin cancer cells. According to this report [11], various forms of reduced calorific intake such as fasting demonstrate a wide range of beneficial effects able to help prevent malignancies and increase the efficacy of cancer prevention.

15. Speeds Healing And Recovery

Exercising while fasting results in increased fat burn and there are some powerful benefits to be gained by combining the two, especially when you can get a solid workout in at the end of your period of not eating.

Some studies [12] have reported that after three weeks of regular overnight fasting, endurance cyclists noted a more rapid post-workout recovery with no decrease in performance. Studies examining weight training in a fasted state showed an increase in the subject's 'cellular anabolic response' to the post-workout meal, indicating that the period of fasting upped some of the body's physiological indicators of muscular growth. Even if these studies aren't entirely conclusive, the healing power of fasting and the improvements to your sleep and eating habits definitely aids the body in recovering from a workout, no matter how intense it is.

16. Triggers Autophagy

This study [13] indicates that one way of inducing autophagy is by food restriction, which regulates autophagy in many organs, including the liver. It has further been proven that during a fast, the body's cells begin to undertake a process called autophagy. Over time, dysfunctional or damaged proteins can build up within cells, and this waste removal process helps the body filter out this excess material. This process is an important part of the body's ability to repair and detoxify. Some researchers assert that increased autophagy offers a boost in protection from a number of diseases, including cancer and Alzheimer's disease. Autophagy helps cells overcome stresses brought on from external causes like the deprivation of important nutrients, as well as internal issues like pathogens or invading infectious organisms.

17. Promotes Anti-Aging Hormone

If you're over the age of 30 and especially if you lead a sedentary lifestyle, you've likely entered a phase known as somatopause (or age-related growth hormone deficiency). According to this article [14], the natural production of growth hormone starts to declines in our twenties, leading to a reduction in lean body mass and bone mineral density and an increase in body fat, especially abdominal fat. As growth hormone declines over time, a person begins to look and feel older. However, fasting sets in motion a hormonal chain of events that not only burns fat but also protects hard-earned muscle. It has been proven that after approximately sixteen to twenty-four hours in a fasted state, our bodies release a massive surge of growth hormone. One study showed that while fasting for twenty-four hours, human growth hormone increased an average of 1,300 per cent in women and nearly 2,000 per cent in men. But, please note, depending on each individual makeup, others may find that they begin to lose muscle with fasts that are longer than twenty-four hours, so each person is unique and it is important to listen to your body and do what works for you. Personally, the longest fast I have done is seventy-two hours and it was just an experiment to see how I would feel. Surprisingly, because my body was already fat adapted at that time, thus it had already become efficient in using the stored fat for energy, I felt energized and did not even feel hungry and I was able to perform my workouts during my closed window. It is always important to listen to your body. When you feel very hungry, Just Eat until your body gets used to the fasting protocol.

Another activity that can lead to a dramatic increase in growth hormone is high-intensity interval exercises. Combining fasting with high intensity exercise can provide synergistic effects to boost growth hormone and the presence of growth hormone in adulthood leads to a healthier body composition.

Some of the benefits of growth hormone:

- Keeps your body lean
- Increases synthesis of new protein tissues to promote muscle recovery and repair
- Decreases fat accumulation
- Strengthens bones
- Protects your organs from the decline that occurs with age
- Promotes healthy hair and nail growth
- Improves circulation
- Gives a more favorable cholesterol profile
- Decreases signs and symptoms of aging

Furthermore, fasting signals to your cells that it's time to focus the body's energy on conserving, restoring and repairing your body's internal machinery. It's easier if you think of fasting as 'cleanse' mode, where your cells scavenge your body for free radicals, agents of disease and damaged cells and recycle them to conserve energy. Thanks to autophagy, it basically means your body is efficiently recycling and cleaning the damaged cells.

18. Fasting Can Trigger Stem Cell, Immune Regeneration

According to Australian spinal research foundations article [15], short-term fasting seems to have made a resurgence in popularity in recent years, with IF being used for more than just weight loss. The article points to research which reveals that fasting even twice a week could significantly lower the risk of developing Parkinson's and Alzheimer's disease and can trigger stem cell regeneration and help reboot damaged immune systems. These findings were a result of two studies led by Professor Valter Longo of the USC longevity institute at USC Leonard Davis School of Gerontology.

How does the fasting/immune system connection work? "It gives the 'OK' for stem cells to go ahead and begin proliferating and rebuild the entire system," says Professor Longo. "And the good news is that the body gets rid of the parts of the system that might be damaged, old and inefficient during the fasting. Now, if you start with a system heavily damaged by chemotherapy or aging, fasting cycles can literally generate a new immune system." See more here: (www. telegraph.co.uk/science/2016/03/12/fasting-for-three-days-can-regenerate-entire-immune-system-study/) [16].

The article indicates that the body is forced to use stores of glucose and fat during prolonged fasting, but it also breaks down a significant portion of white blood cells. This depletion "triggers stem cell-based regeneration of new immune system cells". It essentially shifts stem cells from a dormant state into a state of self-renewal. Prior researches had also shown that short-term fasts starve cancer cells and facilitate the chemo drug therapies to better target the cancer.

Though this is potentially the big news, fasting for long periods of time or sometimes even regular shorter fasts should be done with caution, and with the guidance of a suitable health professional.

Chapter 6

Methods Of Intermittent Fasting And Recommendations

I will discuss the six most popular common methods of IF, though there are many other methods available. Different methods will yield different results for different people. Do not force yourself to follow a particular method because you will not be able to sustain it. It is better to choose a yielding method or protocol that suits your lifestyle and meets your personal goals. Note that each protocol has its own guidelines. I will therefore highlight these methods and some recommendations on how to break the fast whilst following this lifestyle.

I. Sixteen-Hour Fast/Eight-Hour Feed Or Lean Gains (16:8) [17]

Started by Martin Berkhan and best for

dedicated gym-goers who want to lose body fat and build muscle, the Lean gains approach is pretty straightforward: you eat all your daily meals within an eight-hour window and fast the other sixteen hours of the day. During the fasting window you restrict anything with any calorific content. During my self-experimentation, I mostly used this protocol during weekends and special occasions since it has a wider open window. With this style of fasting, you would stop eating after dinner around 7 or 8pm. When you wake up the following morning, instead of eating breakfast, you would have coffee, tea or water and have your late breakfast around 11am or 12pm as your first meal. On this schedule, most people move forward their breakfast and sometimes they choose to skip the morning meal every day and have lunch as their first meal. But how many meals you eat within that eight-hour window is your choice. Some people choose to eat two meals during that window whilst others choose to eat three. At the time when I was following this protocol, during the fasting period, I consumed no calories except black coffee or tea with no sugar or milk in the morning followed by water for the entire day. (Other practitioners include calorie-free sweeteners, diet soda, sugar-free gum, lemon or a splash of milk in their coffee.

However, everyone is different and I will suggest everyone should do what works for them.) This method is easier when a person chooses to fast through the night and into the morning and you can adapt it to your lifestyle. What and when you eat during the feeding window also depends on your fitness and health goals. However, regardless of your specific program, whole, unprocessed foods should make up the majority of your food intake if you have weight loss and healthy living as your objective.

Advantages

A major advantage of the sixteen-hour fast is that it is fairly simple to incorporate into everyday life. For most people, it only means skipping breakfast or pushing breakfast forward to close to 11am or 12pm and eating lunch and dinner within eight hours of each other. Many people do not feel hungry in the morning despite skipping breakfast and therefore find this method extremely easy to implement. The daily sixteen-hour fast certainly has more power than the daily twelve-hour fast, since weight loss on this regimen tends to be slow and steady. That said, most people find breaking it up into three meals easier to stick to, since we are typically already programmed to eat this way, though it is not necessary. You can simply skip breakfast to have lunch and dinner instead. By the way, you can still have your breakfast at noon as your lunch.

Disadvantages

Even though there is flexibility in **when** you eat, Lean gains has pretty specific guidelines of **what** to eat, especially in relation to when you're working out. The strict nutrition plan and scheduling meals perfectly around workouts can make the program a bit tougher to adhere to if you are regularly working out, as sometimes you might want to eat post-workout.

I have, however, found the 16:8 fasting and feeding structure to possess a natural flow and easy to start with since it is not that disruptive to everyday life. Though I exercised regularly, I still kept my fast limited to plain coffee and water whilst waiting for my window to open.

2. Twenty-Hour Fasts/Four-Hour Feed (20:4) Or The 'Warrior Diet' [18]

Started by Ori Hofmekler, this approach is best suited to people who like following rules. This is my favorite method hence I call it "my sweet spot."

The warrior diet requires you to follow your instincts when it comes to eating. This eating plan does not restrict you to counting calories and macronutrients. The ancient warriors normally had little to no food during the day and ate their prey at night. Ori Hofmekler advocates controlled fasting and exercising on a virtually empty stomach. You ease into restricting your food intake to only one meal a day. If you adapt to this eating plan, it is said that you will be better or more efficient at burning fat for fuel and will have greater energy and also be lean. Warriors in training can expect to fast for about twenty hours every day and eat one large meal every night within four hours.

When practicing this protocol, I found success mostly when I fasted clean, that is, having plain black coffee, no sugar, no milk and drinking plain water. Other practitioners still find success in eating a few servings of raw fruit or vegetables, fresh juice, or a few servings of protein during the closed window. However, this will not be a true fast since this could lead to raised insulin levels. This eating protocol is supposed to maximize the sympathetic nervous system's 'fight or flight' response, which is intended to promote alertness, boost energy, and stimulate fat burning. The four-hour eating window which Hofmekler refers to as the "overeating" phase is at night in order to maximize the parasympathetic nervous system's ability to help the body recuperate, promoting calm, relaxation and digestion, while also allowing the body to use the nutrients consumed for repair and growth. Eating at night may also help the body produce hormones and burn fat during the day, according to Hofmekler. During these four hours, the order in which you eat specific food groups matters, too. Hofmekler advises one to start with vegetables, protein and fat. After finishing those groups, and only if you are still hungry, you may tack on some carbohydrates. I have never been strict with following this order of eating; however, my body usually responded well whenever I opened the window with a fruit or a vegetable. The essence of the matter is to always listen to your body.

Advantages

Many have gravitated towards this way of eating because the 'fasting' period still allows you to eat a few small tasty snacks, which can make it easier to get through the day. As the methodology explains, many practitioners experience high energy levels and an enormous amount of fat loss.

Disadvantages

This way of eating might prove to be a challenge for those who prefer not to eat large meals late in the day. As I previously said, it is always important to choose and try to experiment with what works for you.

Personally, I experiment and sometimes combine different protocols to see what works for me. With time, I have found this lifestyle most practical with a few adjustments to suit my personal goals and lifestyle. Always remember that everyone is different and it is important to change things around to find what works for you. I always preferred a clean fast for a minimum of twenty hours and for the next four hours or less I would then eat whatever I liked.

3. Fast-5 (19:5) [19]

This lifestyle encouraged by Dr Bert Herring, encourages the practitioner to eat within five consecutive hours. It does not mean eat constantly for five hours, neither does it mean eat as much as you can. During the five consecutive hours, eat as much as you are hungry for and eat what you want to eat. Consuming liquids with calorie content counts as eating, so only calorie-free beverages are permitted during the fasting period, so no juice, protein shakes, fruit etc. As long as you observe at least a nineteen-hour fast daily and eat within five or fewer consecutive hours, you are within the guidelines of the Fast-5 program. Dr Bert says that there are two ways to start: 'cold turkey' and a gradual 'adjustment' approach.

- Cold Turkey

  With this approach, you choose not to eat until the eating window opens. It is always important to remember that if you slip and do not reach your target fasting hours, don't give up. Getting close to your goal pushes your body to adapt, which can make it easier to reach your goal on your next try. Slips are a normal part of adjustment.

- Adjustment

tIn the adaptation approach (extensively described in *The Fast-5 Diet and Fast 5-Lifestyle by Dr. Bert Herring*) the time one first eats (called 'break-fast' to avoid confusion with breakfast) is gradually pushed back. The time of break-fast is pushed back by the same interval (half an hour or an hour) every day or every few days until it is the desired window opening time.

'Ratchet' Adjustment

Dr Herring mentions that one can also adapt using the faster 'ratchet' approach, in which you don't eat until at least fifteen minutes later than yesterday's break-fast time, but if you are not hungry at that time you will wait until you are. With this approach, you postpone break-fast by whatever time increment your body is ready for. On some days, break-fast may be fifteen minutes later than the day before, and on other days it may be an hour or more later, but it does not fall back.

The Fast-5 way of eating is said to work because it restores appetite to an appropriate level for the amount of stored energy (fat) you have and the amount of energy you expend in a day. You take in less food so your body burns fat.

4. Twenty-Four-Hour Fasts Or Eat Stop Eat (24) [20]

Started by Brad Pilon, this is best for healthy eaters looking for an extra boost.

Pilon's plan involves fasting up to two times a week and it does not require you to give up any specific food group. Eat Stop Eat works in a simple way. You fast once or twice a week, aiming for a complete break from food for twenty-four hours at a time. For example, you might eat normally until 8pm on a Monday then fast until Tuesday 8pm, resuming normal eating at that time. If it is not possible to keep a twenty-four-hour fast, Pilon says twenty to twenty-four hours will also work. For the next couple of days a woman may eat approximately 2,000 calories (2,500 calories for a man) and on this plan you are not expected to fast for consecutive days. After the normal eating days you can consider another fast and repeat the process.

I like doing a twenty-four-hour fast, especially after a weekend or a special occasion, for a minimum of twice a week and thereafter revert to my 20:4 during the week and 16:8 on weekends for my maximum fasting health benefits. As we discussed, with this eating plan you fast for twenty-four hours once or twice per week (which creator Brad Pilon prefers to call a '24-hour break from eating'). No food is consumed, but you can drink calorie-free beverages. After the fast is over, you then go back to eating normally. "Act like you didn't fast," Pilon says. "Some people need to finish the fast at a normal mealtime with a big meal, while others are OK ending the fast with an afternoon snack. Time your meals the way that works best for you, and remember to adjust your timing as your schedule changes," he says. Eating this way still does not limit what you are able to eat, just how often, according to Eat Stop Eat. It is important to note that incorporating regular workouts, particularly resistance training, is key to succeed on this plan if weight loss or improved body composition are your main goals.

Advantages

While twenty-four hours may seem like a long time to go without food, the good news is that this program is flexible. You don't have to go all-or-nothing at the beginning. You can choose to go as long as you can without food the first day and gradually increase the fasting phase over time to help your body adjust. Pilon suggests starting the fast when you are busy, and on a day where you have no eating obligations like a work lunch or happy hour. This fasting regimen has several important advantages compared to other longer fasts. Because you still eat a meal on the fasting day, you can take any medications that must be taken with food when you open your eating window. What I generally appreciate about IF is that there are no forbidden foods and no counting calories, weighing food or restricting your diet, which makes it easier to make it a permanent lifestyle. That said, this isn't a free-for-all, therefore, one needs to exercise moderation and be reasonable especially if one has fitness and health goals.

Disadvantages

Going twenty-four hours without any calories may be too difficult for some, especially at first. Many people struggle with going extended periods of time with no food, citing annoying symptoms such as headaches, fatigue, or feeling cranky or anxious. Usually these side effects diminish over time. At times, others find because of the long fasting period they are more tempted to binge. This then requires a lot of self-control, which some people lack.

Personally, I found that I could easily mix this protocol with my other weekly protocols. Considering the fact that during the day, my family is all away and I am usually working, the twenty- to twenty-four-hour fasts make it easier for me to enjoy my one meal a day, usually dinner with family later in the evening. So it allows me to fast without disrupting family dinners since it is about skipping breakfast and lunch. It's particularly easy during a busy day at work since I would normally start my mornings with a cup of coffee, skipping breakfast, then work right through lunch and get home to prepare family dinner. The fact that I am able to eat anything my family is eating makes this lifestyle effortless and saves both time and money. Thinking of the three-course dinner which I will have, keeps me motivated to delay my eating to later.

Nutrient deficiency is not a major concern with a twenty-four-hour fast since you are still eating daily, you just need to make sure that during that meal you aim to consume adequate proteins, vitamins and minerals by eating nutrient-dense, natural, unprocessed foods.

5. The Diet Also Known As 'The 5:2 Fast Diet' [21]

Popularized by Dr Michael Mosley MD and Mimi Spencer, it is best for those who don't mind counting calories and who prefer to have some non-fasting days. The basic concept behind the fast diet is to eat normally for five days per week and eat very restricted calories on the other two days. In this way of eating, it is recommended that the fasting days should not be back to back. One is advised to have at least one normal eating day in between the fasting days. Rather than completely abstaining from food for a period of time, this diet calls for a period of low calorific intake. On the two 'fast' days, women may eat up to 500 calories per day and men up to 600 calories. You can choose whichever two days of the week you prefer to fast, as long as there is at least one non-fasting day in between. The 500 to 600 calories can be consumed in a single meal or spread out into multiple meals over the course of a day. Though of course, they would be very small meals.

Advantages

It sounds like it is easier to follow since one fasts for only two days a week.

Disadvantages

Eating 500–600 calories for a couple of days a week can be very tough. A person will miss other benefits associated with clean fasting.

6. Alternate Day Fasting Or Up Day Down Day Diet

Popularized by Dr Krista Varady, this consists of one day of unregulated eating followed by a day of eating 500 calories or less. If you are ambitious, you can do your alternate day as a full twenty-four-hour fast. This plan is mostly best for disciplined dieters with a specific goal weight. The idea is that you severely restrict the number of calories you eat on fasting days while eating however you would like on non-fasting days. You do not completely cut out food on fasting days but it is severely restricted. The recommended amount is about 25 per cent of whatever your total calories on a normal day would be. For example, if you have determined that 2,000 calories a day is the amount you require to lose weight, on a fasting day you only eat 500 calories. I have never tried this fasting protocol since it reminds me of my dieting days. I have made a decision to live and simply enjoy my meals until I am satisfied. I have decided to stop counting calories and measuring and weighing my food.

Advantages

This method is all about weight loss, so if that's your main goal, this one would be ideal to take a closer look at. On average, those who cut calories by 20 to 35 per cent typically achieve a loss of about two and a half pounds per week, according to Johnson. However, remember that everyone is different. There will always be different results for different people.

Disadvantages

Counting and dieting mentality comes into play. If like me you simply want a hassle-free lifestyle, you might not find this way of eating appealing. While the method is pretty easy to follow, it can be easy to binge on the 'normal' day. The best way to stay on track is planning your meals ahead of time as often as possible. Then you're not caught at the drive-through or all-you-can-eat buffet with a grumbling belly.

Important Points To Remember

- It takes our bodies time to adjust, and some require more time than others.
- Be cautious at first, and start slowly with a shorter fast.
- While these methods are the best known in terms of integrating periods of fasting into your eating schedule, there are many other similar philosophies based on meal timing, including longer fasts for a few days or even weeks.
- Fasting, regardless of the method, isn't for everyone. If you have any medical conditions or special dietary requirements, it's important to consult your doctor before giving IF a try.

- Anyone who tries it should also plan to listen to their bodies while fasting. If it's not agreeing with you, or if you need to eat a little something to tide you over, that's just fine. **Just Eat.**
- Keep in mind that hormones and our individual gut health can make it harder for some to get results similar to others. Therefore, do not compare your meals, weight loss or general progress with that of the next person. What is working for another person might not necessarily work for you.
- You are likely to experience loss in centimeters/inches before kilograms/pounds. Centimeters seem to disappear before the weight comes off. This is probably due to fat distribution and means you will typically see loosening of belts and pants before the weight loss is seen on the scale.
- You will likely feel cool or cold during the fasting period due to the absence of heat generated as a by-product of digestion of the usual meals, according to Dr Bert. Digestion is a metabolic activity, but the energy burned by digesting food is less than the energy that gets stored, resulting in a net gain of calories and fat. While the absence of digestive heat may mean wearing an extra layer in cold

weather, it also means greater comfort in warm or hot weather.

- Listen to your body, trust the process and focus on your 'study of one'. It is always prudent to be cautious at first. If it doesn't make you feel better, try something different, or accept the fact that maybe fasting isn't for you. Keep on tweaking until you find what works for you.

- This lifestyle does not require unnecessary rigid rules, always making it feel like a chore to skip a meal or two. IF is a free and flexible lifestyle not a life sentence. **Just Eat.**

Avoid making people around feel like your lifestyle is nothing but torture and self-deprivation. Enjoy your meal times and remember to always give your metabolism or body a break. That is the basic essence of IF. IF is just like exercising. When you first start to lift weights, for example, your muscles are very sore afterward. This is expected and should not dissuade you from continuing to work out – and over time, as you grow stronger, you can lift the same weight without difficulty or soreness. Similarly, with IF, the initial period may be difficult, but things get easier with practice. Fit IF into your own life. This is the most important tip I can offer and it has the greatest impact on whether you stick to your fasting regimen or not. Do not change your life to fit your fasting schedule – change your fasting schedule to fit your life. Don't limit yourself socially because you're fasting. Always remember that there will be times during which it's difficult or even impossible to fast, such as vacations, holidays and weddings. Do not try to force fasting into these celebrations if it is not possible to accommodate it. These occasions are times to relax and enjoy yourself. What better way to do this than through eating together as a family and with friends. Bonding and laughing over a delicious meal is invaluable especially in this modern, busy world. You can simply increase your next fasting times to compensate or you can just resume your regular fasting schedule. The Golden Rule: *Adjust your fasting schedule to what makes sense for your goals and lifestyle.*

Caution:

If you have a medical condition, then you should consult with your doctor before trying IF. This is particularly important if you:

- Have diabetes
- Have problems with blood sugar regulation
- Have low blood pressure
- Take medication
- Are underweight
- Have a history of eating disorders
- Are a female who is trying to conceive
- Are a female with a history of amenorrhea
- Are pregnant or breastfeeding

All that being said, IF does have an outstanding safety profile. There is nothing 'dangerous' about not eating for a while if you are healthy and well-nourished overall.

Chapter 7

My Success In Combining Exercise With Intermittent Fasting

When talking about health and fitness, most people focus on what workout they should do and how hard they must train. The truth is, as I have mentioned before, training is only 20 per cent of the whole picture and the other 80 per cent is to do with the food we eat.

One of the best ways to boost your return on your exercise investment is to do your workout while fasting. When you combine exercise with IF, it essentially forces your body to shed excess fat. Your body's fat-burning processes are controlled by your sympathetic nervous system (SNS) and your SNS is activated by exercise and lack of food. The combination of fasting and exercising maximizes the impact of cellular factors and catalysts which force the breakdown of fat and glycogen or energy. Another reason is that fasting can trigger a dramatic rise in the production of human growth hormone (HGH), also known as 'the fitness hormone'. Recent research found fasting raised production by 1,300 per cent in women and 2,000 per cent in men. The combination of fasting and exercising maximizes the impact of cellular factors and catalysts which force the breakdown of fat and glycogen for energy.

Exercising and fasting together yield acute stress, which actually benefits the muscles. According to fitness expert Ori Hofmekler, acute states of oxidative stress are: *"essential for keeping muscle machinery tuned. Technically, acute stress, oxidative stress makes the muscles increasingly resilient to oxidative stress. It stimulates glutathione and SOD (superoxide dismutase, the first antioxidant mobilized by the cells for defense) production in the mitochondria along with increased muscular capacity to utilize energy, generate force and resist fatigue. Hence, exercise and fasting helps to counteract all the main determinants of muscle aging. But, there is something else about exercise and fasting. When combined, they trigger a mechanism that recycles and rejuvenates the brain and muscle tissues."*

The mechanism he refers to triggers genes and growth factors, including brain-derived neurotropic factor (BDNF) and muscle regulatory factors (MRFs). These factors signal brain stem cells and muscular satellite cells to convert into new neurons and new muscle cells, respectively.

When I started to experiment with IF, my initial purpose was to lose weight and body fat, but then I started to delve deeper and found other advantages and benefits which made me want to continue this lifestyle even after achieving my target size or goal body. IF lifestyle has helped me drop body fat percentage and increase muscle mass. Interestingly, hunger is not much of a problem as I have shifted to regulate my fat-burning enzymes.

I always exercise in a fasted state with ease and I have metabolically adapted to using the stored fat for fuel. My previous fitness assessment always showed adequate lean muscle however the fat percentage was always too high. My fat percentage was always on the very obese category irrespective of my regular exercise. These results always confused me since I was exercising regularly at least six to eight hours per week and eating three healthy meals and two healthy snacks per day. Little did I know that weight loss and gain is attributable to the times I was eating.

Five to six meals a day did not work for me hence always finding myself on the heavy end of the scale. I thought this was muscle but how wrong I was – it was excess stored fat.

Yes, muscle gain and loss is also an important function of exercise. Exercise is the best way to build strong muscles. As such, exercise remains an important aspect in building and retaining lean muscle mass. To make sure that I retained my muscle mass whilst following this lifestyle, I ensured that I incorporated both cardio and resistance training into my IF lifestyle.

I have come to appreciate the fact that meals and exercise serve different purposes in my body. It does not make sense to then conclude that if I fast my body will eat muscle. Why should my body eat muscle when fasting whilst on the other hand it has a lot of unused energy stored in my body as fat? It should then be pretty obvious that when the body runs out of immediate available energy it should resort to the energy that has been stored for many years as fat, not to the muscle. Since the body stores excess energy as fat, it should turn to the stored fat during the time of need. The exception will be if one is underweight or has the lowest body fat percentage and in those instances fasting for fat loss would not be necessary. Remember that the body is able to retain lean tissue during fasting due to the presence of Human Growth Hormone which plays a big role in maintaining lean muscle during fasting. When hormonal changes take place to give us more energy they keep glucose and energy stores high whilst maintaining our lean muscle and keeping bones healthy due to the growth hormone.

Human Growth Hormone

Let us take some time and look closely at what Human Growth Hormone really is. The body naturally produces growth hormone (HGH or GH) in the pituitary gland and it is responsible for cell growth and regeneration. Increasing muscle mass and bone density is impossible without HGH but it also plays a major role in maintaining the health of all human tissue, including that of the brain and other vital organs. When secreted, HGH remains active in the blood stream for only a few minutes but this is enough time for the liver to convert it into growth factors. Human Growth Hormone can turn back the body's internal clock thus helping a person to rapidly build muscle, burn fat and increase the body's overall energy. It has been proven that fasting enhances growth hormone secretion. Studies have shown that when a person is in a fed state, HGH levels are frequently unpredictable. As discussed, fasting has a positive dramatic impact on HGH levels. Increased

HGH results in greater endurance with faster muscle repair and growth as well as slowing the aging process. One study showed that interval training while fasting increased HGH by 1,300 per cent in women and 2,000 per cent in men.

Is Breakfast Really The Most Important Meal Of The Day?

For decades, we have been told that breakfast is the most important meal of the day. It was said, if you skip breakfast you will get fat, make poorer food choices, have no energy and eat more overall. Research has shown that some of these things are likely true due to certain circumstances. For instance, if you skip breakfast you are more likely to buy food that is inherently unhealthy before lunch. However, in terms of energy, I felt no discernible loss at any time throughout my study of one. On the contrary, when in a fasted state, I usually feel a greater sense of mental clarity and my immune system improved. I can actually sometimes read without my reading glasses as my eyesight is so much better, thanks to the low sugar levels and autophagy. Ever since embarking on this lifestyle I experience an overwhelming amount of energy during my workouts, my body easily switches to stored fat for energy when the need arises.

My Exercise Routine Is More Enjoyable And Fun

My fitness regime has never been as easy, enjoyable and laid back as it is now. After spending years doing eight to twelve hours of exercise per week to help me burn more calories in order to keep my weight in check, exercise is now mostly for fun, fitness, enjoyment and health benefits. Indoor cycling is my passion, I enjoy taking long walks and riding my outdoor bike with my son for fun. As for my muscle strength, resistance training is my go-to exercise. After depleting my body fat cells, building more muscle is very important to give me a great physique and rev up my metabolism all the time. I don't panic if I 'miss a workout', as I used to do. My basic understanding is that the times I choose to eat has the biggest impact on my overall physique. This knowledge has empowered me and my main focus in now on *when* I eat. It has become evident to me that staying active and eating at the right times is absolutely an important part of any healthy lifestyle.

My interest is mainly on the effects of fasting on my insulin levels. It became evident that insulin resistance has been a contributing factor to my obesity. My body cells were essentially ignoring insulin as it rings the doorbell to deliver energy (glucose) to the body cells. IF and regular exercise has significantly normalized my insulin sensitivity. On the other hand, leptin, the hormone that regulates fat storage as well as hunger signals, and ghrelin, another hormone that tells the brain that the body is hungry, can also be normalized by the process of fasting, hence appetite correction. Leptin is produced by fat cells and works by telling the brain to turn off hunger signals when the body fat levels are sufficient for survival and reproduction. Leptin is part of the reason why low-fat diets hardly ever work and usually result in the dieter being hungry all time. Surprisingly, it has been shown that overweight people have very high levels of leptin, yet they are still always hungry. The body is telling the brain to stop eating but the brain has become deaf to the signals because of over-exposure to high levels of leptin. Fasting allows the brain to 'hear' the body's requests for insulin and leptin.

Chapter 8

What Happens To Fat Cells During Weight Loss?

During the period of self-experimentation, I become curious about what really happens when a person loses fat. I wondered what happens to the fat cells when they are emptied and have become smaller. My research led me to a very interesting and informative realization and I'd like to share this with you. When we think about our weight, it is often tied to how much fat we have in our bodies and it is important to remember that we all need some fat. Fat is an important component of the cell membrane, it is a place to store energy, some vitamins and it is used to make different hormones that we need to transmit throughout the body.

According to the *International Journal of Oral Science* [22], while fat (white adipose tissue, WAT) is often associated with the development of type-2 diabetes, it is essential for energy homeostasis because it stores excess energy and releases lipids in response to energy deficits. However, modern lifestyle favors longer periods of daily energy intake and shorter fasting periods. This erratic eating pattern is associated with metabolic disadvantages and contributes to the current global obesity and diabetic epidemic. Fasting brings various positive health impacts, suggesting that modulation of fasting periods can be used as therapeutic intervention. The journal also states that IF provides beneficial effects against aging, cancer, cardiovascular diseases and neurodegenerative diseases.

On average, fat percentage above 25 per cent for men and 30 per cent for women can be a health hazard. This is especially the case if it is stored in our upper bodies or around our internal organs which can cause many problems, ranging from increased risk of diabetes, to heart diseases and cancer. Fat is stored inside the fat cell in the form of triacylglycerol and we should also note that fat is not burned right there in the fat cell, it is, instead liberated from the fat cells through hormonal pathways. When stimulated to do so, the fat simply releases its contents triacylglycerol, into the bloodstream as free fatty acids (FFAs), and these will then be transported through the blood to the body tissues where the energy is needed. A typical young male adult is said to store about 60,000 to 100,000 calories of energy in body fat cells.

Therefore, when your body needs energy because there is an energy deficit, the body releases hormones and enzymes that signal your fat cells to release your fat reserves instead of keeping them in storage. For stored fat to be liberated from fat cells, hydrolysis (lipolysis or fat breakdown) splits the molecule of triacylglycerol into glycerol and three fatty acids. An important enzyme called hormone sensitive lipase (HSL) is the catalyst for this reaction. The stored fat or energy gets released into the bloodstream as free fatty acids and these free fatty acids will then be shuttled off to the muscles where the energy is needed. As blood flow increases to the active muscles, more FFAs are delivered to the muscles that need them. An important enzyme called lipoprotein lipase (LPL) then helps the FFAs get into the mitochondria of the muscle cell where the FFAs can be burnt for energy. These mitochondria form the cellular 'powerhouse', where energy production takes place and it's where the FFAs go to be burnt for energy.

When the FFAs are released from the fat cell, the fat cell would normally shrink and that is why a person always looks leaner after losing body fat. The fat cells have simply gotten smaller. A small or empty fat cell is what we are all after so that we can look lean and have a defined beautiful look. It was once believed that the number of fat cells could not increase or decrease. However, it has been noticed that fat cells can indeed increase both in size and in number at certain times and under certain circumstances, such as:

- During late childhood and early puberty
- During pregnancy
- During adulthood when an extreme amount of weight is gained

However, it is important to note that some people are genetically predisposed to have more fat cells than others and women have more fat cells than men. An infant usually has about 5 to 6 billion fat cells. The number increases during early childhood and puberty. A healthy adult with normal body composition has about 25 to 30 billion fat cells. A typical overweight adult has around 75 billion fat cells. In case of severe obesity this number can be as high as 250 to 300 billion fat cells. The average size (weight) of an adult fat cell is about 0.6 micrograms but they can vary in size from 0.6 micrograms to 0.9 micrograms. On the other hand, an overweight person's fat cells can be up to three times larger than a person with ideal body composition. Remember, the body's fat is basically a reserve source of energy and fat cells are like storage tanks. These fat cell tanks can expand or shrink in size depending on how filled they are. Like a balloon fills with air, fat cells expand when filled with fat. The fat cell starts as a nearly empty fat storage tank when a person is lean. However, any excess energy is stored as fat and this is when the fat cells fill up and stretch out as much as they can. When you lose weight you don't actually lose fat cells. Rather, they simply shrink or empty themselves out. An IF and exercise lifestyle will go a long way in helping you burn your excess stored fat and build muscle.

As discussed, fat is basically a store of energy and when you need it you break down the fat into FFAs which then go into the liver for energy. When you have excess fat, it generates so much FFA that the liver cannot handle it and as a result it stores it. This triggers a host of problems including non-alcoholic fatty liver diseases, insulin resistance, diabetes and many other health challenges. When you eat food, you provide your body with relatively large amounts of energy in a short period of time. The body will burn a portion of this energy and store the excess energy as body fat for later use. The scientific term for this period of nutrient absorption and processing is called postprandial. Post means 'after' and prandial means 'having to do with a meal'. While in this postprandial (which means after eating) or 'fed state', no fat burning occurs since the body is in a fat storage mode due to high insulin levels. The body does not see any need to burn stored fat for energy since you have just provided it with all it needs plus more. Eventually your body finishes processing and absorbing the food which can take six to eight hours and thereafter it enters in to the post-absorptive state. The energy provided by food is now gone but the body still needs to function, therefore to meet those energy demands the body turns to the stored fat. The body must now shift into fat-burning mode to survive whilst it is waiting for the next meal. That is when the benefits of IF come into action since the fat cells are now challenged to empty themselves and this is only possible if you delay your next meal for a few hours after the post-absorptive stage. Every day your body moves in and out of postprandial – post absorptive – fat storing – fat burning states. The fat lowering capabilities of IF is said to be caused in part by the modulating hormone, leptin. The accumulation of fat within the fat cells causes the fat cell to secrete leptin. Leptin then signals to the brain to decrease appetite and food intake. So when leptin signaling is working properly, extra fat in your fat cells will cause a surge in leptin, telling the brain to stop eating to avoid further fat gain. Unfortunately, the leptin's ability to decrease food consumption can be overwhelmed by excess continuous eating leading to excess body fat.

I am neither a scientist nor a medical doctor, so I have tried to summarize this in the most simplistic way possible for ease of understanding.

In a nutshell:

- During IF, insulin goes down and the body has the opportunity to tap into fat stores for energy. Insulin sensitivity is important for the acceleration of fat loss and everything you can do to improve it should be a priority.
- If you are gaining weight and it's going up beyond control, make a decision to stop right now as your fat cells might be multiplying making it difficult to burn fat in the future. Take action now and turn your body into a fat-burning machine through IF.
- If you have already lost weight you must be forever careful and diligent since your fat cells are not gone, they have merely shrunk and emptied out. IF is not a fad diet with an end date. Instead, it is a permanent lifestyle which will always give your body the time to tap into the fat stores and convert them into energy. Always note that if you want to stay lean, it will be a good decision to consider adopting this way of eating forever.
- If, after achieving your ideal weight or goal

size, you choose to go back to your former eating habits, always visualize what might be happening to your fat cells since they are still there and these fat cells can expand at any time.

- Genetics should not always be used as an excuse. Though genetics can, to some extent, be a cause of obesity in some, always remember that the past is not an excuse and neither is your present condition. You can either make excuses or get the results but you cannot do both. You may not have control over how many fat cells you were born with but you do have control over how much fat deposit you store in your fat cells. Have a look at your lifestyle, exercise routine, eating patterns and your mental attitude. You are the boss of your own life and the decisions you make. It is counterproductive to think of yourself as a victim of circumstances beyond your control.

Just Eat And Then Stop Eating!

Chapter 9

How To Begin Intermittent Fasting And What To Expect

IF is best approached as a shift in lifestyle and eating patterns, rather than just another diet. What I enjoy mostly about IF is the fact that I do not have to count calories, measure my portions or weigh anything. My focus is mainly to simply eat food that nourishes my body (making sure to include all the major food groups, of course) and enjoy some treats, in moderation.

To start the process, take small steps at first. While there are many fasting protocols one can adopt, the one that I found to be the easiest is described below.

Start off by skipping early breakfast and then not eating anything until noon. If you finished your last meal by 8pm the previous day, you will have fasted for sixteen hours. Then, allow yourself eight hours within which to eat your lunch and dinner, making sure to finish dinner by 8pm. In this way, you will have completed a 16:8 protocol – that's sixteen hours of fasting (the 'closed window') and eight hours during which you may eat (the 'open window').

This sixteen-hour closed window is a good starting point because for the first few hours after finishing your last meal you will be full and then, most likely, asleep for a further six to eight hours. So, by the time you wake up, even if you feel hungry, you know that you only have a few hours to get through before you can eat again. Not only that, but your body will have already started to turn to your fat reserves for its energy, so you must simply remember this if you feel tempted to have a snack, or else this fat-burning process will stop. If you really need to consume something, try a cup of black coffee or tea (no sugar). Water is also very good. (See below for further tips.)

You will get plenty of benefits by taking it slow at first and then, as you get used to the routine, you can gradually increase your closed window. Please note that it may take a few days, weeks or even months for your body to get the message that you are serious about making it burn fat. Everyone is unique, with different genes, metabolism, levels of internal repair and gut health, so you should not expect the same results at the same time as any other person. Focus on you and you alone.

Once your body clearly gets the idea that it must burn fat for energy, it will begin increasing its production of fat-burning enzymes and turn into a fat-burning machine. (We use the term 'fat adaptation' to describe when the body becomes efficient in utilizing its own fat for energy.)

Pay attention to your body by listening to it and carefully evaluating your own personal situation and needs. If you are already healthy and eating well, IF can be the one thing you need to breakthrough a plateau and take your health, weight loss and performance to the next level.

If you want to start this lifestyle, the following tips might be useful:

- **Drink water**: Staying well-hydrated will make the fasting periods much easier to get through.
- **Keep your electrolytes balanced**: Electrolytes are vital for the normal functioning of the human body. Fruits and vegetables are good sources of electrolytes. Common electrolytes include sodium, potassium, calcium and bicarbonate.
- **Nourishing last meal**: Ensure that your

last meal before closing the window is both nourishing and delicious.

- **Fast overnight**: Do yourself a favor and aim to fast through the night. That way, you are sleeping for however many hours is normal for you, leaving less time to distract yourself from hunger pangs.
- **Think positively**: Do not think of fasting as a period of deprivation; think of it, instead, as giving your body a break to do internal cleansing and healing. Above all, it also gives you a break from thinking about what you want to eat next. Feel joyful and be happy that the next meal you are going to have will be anything your heart desires.
- **Stay busy**: Time goes fast when you are busy, so be industrious. Do all those things you have been postponing. De-clutter your home, finish reading that book (or start a new one), do your gardening, join a friend for a walk, or research your new hobby. Don't think of your break time at work as 'lunch break'; give it a new name, such as 'rest break' or even 'gym break'!
- **Give yourself some love – exercise**: Combining IF with consistent exercise will help you get better results. It does not have to be an extreme workout; it can simply be a low-

intensity workout. Aim to work out a minimum of two or three times per week.

If you find that it is easy and you feel good during the fast, then you can try moving on to longer fasting to eating ratios, such as18:6, 20:4, 22:2 or even, if you're feeling really confident, try a twenty-four-hour fast once or twice per week. A shorter open window usually gives your body more time to tap into the stored fat.

My regular protocol is 20:4 and 22:2 during the week and 16:8 on weekends and special occasions.
Another approach is to simply fast whenever it is convenient. Skip meals from time to time when you're not hungry or don't have time to cook. That will give your body a deserved break and an opportunity to self-cleanse.

There is no need to follow a structured IF plan to derive at least some of the benefits. It is always better to experiment with the different approaches and find something that you enjoy and that easily fits in to your schedule. However, it is recommended to start with at least a twelve-hour fast, as anything less than this will prevent the body from adapting to burning its fat reserves.

Plan your first meal (break-fast). Include lean meat or fish, a vegetable, and maybe a fruit, but do not load up on too much grains and starches. Avoid gorging; strive to eat as though you had not fasted.

Use your break from food as an opportunity to enjoy pleasurable, low-key activities you might normally not make time for. A day without food can be a good time to settle the mind as well as the body. It is important to experiment and find something that works for you. Again, remember that each person is different, our metabolism is different, as is our gut health and our genetic make-up.

Handling Cravings

If you find yourself starting to crave food, try these useful activities to distract yourself:

- Go for a short walk.
- Stay hydrated. Sip water or unsweetened herbal or green tea to minimize 'empty stomach' sensations and support detoxification.
- Call a friend or read a book. Watch TV (but avoid this if it usually triggers your desire to eat).
- Still hungry? **Just Eat** and Fast.

Caution

If you have any medical issues or concerns, talk to your healthcare provider before starting a fast. Fasting is not recommended if you are pregnant, nursing, underweight, diabetic, or struggling with mental illness or eating disorders. If you do not feel well on a fast, cut it short.

So now, hopefully, you understand and appreciate the benefits of fasting and it is up to you to decide whether you want to do it or not.

Open-mindedness and a positive attitude are both essential if you want to make a success of this lifestyle. It is not something to be done for a few months and then discarded like every other dieting system.

It is my hope that this lifestyle sets you up for the most liberating, fulfilling and enjoyable future.

I hope to read your success story in the future.

Chapter 10

Frequently Asked Questions

1. What is Intermittent Fasting?

IF is not a conventional diet but rather an easy lifestyle where one can simply alternate periods of eating (open window) and periods of not eating (closed window). One can still eat normal amounts of food, but in a smaller time frame known as your open window. It is simply a plan which guides you as to when you should eat and when you should not eat. Generally you will be spend more time not eating or fasting than you do eating thus giving your body a chance to tap into its stored fat for fuel.

2. How Long Should I Fast For?

It depends. Some methods recommend fourteen to sixteen hours, some recommend twenty-four hours, forty-eight hours, seventy-two hours etc. It is important to note that true fasting does not begin until about twelve to sixteen hours after your last meal. So you can start with twelve hours and gradually build up to longer periods without eating. The key is to make the transition slow and steady as much as possible. Allow your body to become more efficient in using the stored fat for energy. Remember that, what works for one person might not work for you. That is why different fasting times will work differently for different people. Since this is intermittent, thus variable, you can move the times to suit your individual goals and objectives.

Twelve to sixteen hours would be a perfect place to start since it takes approximately twelve hours for the food to be fully processed in the body. Get your body accustomed to this routine for the first few weeks then you can consider increasing the fasting times to thirteen hours, then to fourteen hours, before you realize you will be able to easily fast for eighteen hours or even twenty-four hours.

3. Will I Not Be Hungry?

That depends on each individual. Many people, including myself, are hardly hungry in the morning. Therefore, one can choose a fasting period at a time of day when they are not normally inclined to eat. Don't forget, when your body gets used to converting fat to energy (fat adaptation) you will rarely feel hungry. You may choose to extend the time you stay without food from the time you wake up until you are fully fat adapted.

4. Can I Exercise While Fasting?

Yes. You will burn fat more when exercising in a fasted state. Use your own judgment. There are many different fasting schedules. Most people fast for between twenty and twenty-four hours and do their training at some point during these hours of fasting. Since growth hormone is high, it is said that you will recover faster and build muscle faster in this fasted state. I do all my training in a fasted state. If you feel too hungry or lightheaded, you should cut back on the exercise in fasting times and **Just Eat**.

There is actually a lot of research that supports skipping eating before exercise to maximize your fat-burning potential. This is called 'fasted cardio' and is usually done first thing in the morning before you've had anything to eat. It is thought to be very beneficial for fat burning because the glycogen stores are depleted from fasting while you sleep and so the body is forced to burn fat as energy. From my personal experience, this has worked well and I associate that with the fact that I had sufficient fat stores to be used as energy. Since the body stores unused energy as fat, and again since my fasts were normally less than twenty-four hours, I was confident that the body would successfully convert the stored fat to fuel during my workouts.

5. Should I Make My Children Fast?

Fasting is not recommended for children under 18 years of age. It is better to restrict food containing added sugars. Children's bodies require more nutrients to grow.

6. What Are The Main Differences In Terms Of Effectiveness Of The Different Types Of Fast?

The choice of any fasting protocol is greatly influenced by an individual's objectives. The shorter the fasting times, the less the effectiveness and the greater the need to do it more frequently. For example, a 16:8 IF is often done daily whilst a twenty-four-hour fast could be done twice or three times a week and still be effective. If there are severe insulin resistance issues and other health matters which could be addressed through fasting, longer fasting could be prescribed. However, a person must always consult their doctor before making any major changes in their eating lifestyle. If you are simply using fasting for weight loss, then fasting can still be done as needed for that purpose. There are no negative health consequences to eating only for a shorter time, say four or two hours. For maintenance purposes, shorter fasting times should still be effective.

7. Can I Keep On Switching My Fasting Times Depending On My Schedule?

The word intermittent means 'occurring at irregular intervals'. So you can apply flexibility to your fasting schedule according to what works for you. As you might have noticed, that is how I prefer doing it. Fasting should not dictate your life and I believe it is better to change things around so that the body keeps on guessing, thus reducing the likelihood to adapt and hit a plateau. However, one needs to correctly calculate the actual fasting hours since it is possible for a person to fast for a very few hours or even not to fast sufficiently to allow fat burn. Conversely if a regular fasting routine works better for you, go ahead and do that instead. You're in control!

8. Is It Better To Eat In The Morning, Afternoon Or Evening To Maximize Weight-Loss Benefits From Fasting?

The time of day you eat probably does matter but only a very little. Some people advise eating in the morning, others at night, so there is little consensus. It is important to experiment and see what works for you since everyone is different. Do what works for you and also what fits within your lifestyle and always remember it is a 'study of one'.

9. Can Artificial Sweeteners In My Coffee And Tea Break My Fast?

There is little information on the sugar alcohols in artificial sweeteners, therefore I am unable to say whether these could break the fast or not. However, I feel that when in doubt it is best to avoid these.

10. Can I Take Apple Cider Vinegar During My Fasting Time?

Apple cider vinegar can be allowed. It has been reported to be more effective in improving insulin sensitivity. Two tablespoons mixed with water in the morning or before meals has been said to be effective.

11. Can I Use Whey Protein During My Closed Window?

It is not advisable to use whey protein during your closed window since it is highly processed and will greatly stimulate insulin, so the likelihood of achieving weight loss is minimal.

12. Should I Take A Multivitamin Or Any Other Supplements?

Different people have different approaches. I prefer to take a multivitamin supplement when my window is open, basically to supplement the food that at times might not be very nutritional. However, if a person predominantly eats whole, unprocessed, organic, 'real food', then they might not find multivitamins necessary.

13. Can I Drink Alcohol During My Closed Window?

No. The body will burn the alcohol instead of allowing the body to burn stored sugar and fat. If you want to drink alcohol, do it moderately during your open window.

14. Is It Important To Include Fiber In My Meals?

Fiber can greatly help with protecting insulin spikes, so it is recommended. Additionally, it can also assist with minimizing constipation.

15. I Lost A Lot Of Weight At The Beginning Of My Fasting Lifestyle But Now My Weight Loss Is Slowing. Why?

The initial rapid weight loss you experience is often water. During those first few days or weeks of quick weight loss whilst fasting, your body normally expels the bloating liquid accumulation thus laying the base for effective fat burning as you become fat adapted. After that evens out you will lose weight, however it will not be as fast as it was in the beginning. To burn stored fat usually takes some time so it is important to be patient and trust the process. Still, to see all of the weight come off the body so quickly is truly a tremendous experience and it provides motivation to keep going. If, however, you are not getting the weight-loss results you desire, try changing your protocol. Try extending your closed window. There is no best fasting protocol since everyone is different. The advice is to experiment with yourself so as to find the fasting protocol that most suits you and gives you your desired results.

16. Why Do I Tend To Crave More Real Food After Fasting?

Fasting has been called a 'reset' button for your sense of taste as the body and palate get cleansed of chemicals and impurities, giving you a keener ability to taste food and more fully enjoy the true flavors of simple foods. There will be many foods that hold less appeal after the fast, especially highly processed foods and those containing too many chemicals, which you will notice more clearly.

17. Can Women Fast During Pregnancy And After Birth Whilst Breastfeeding?

It is not recommended. The mother and the baby need specific nutrients and minerals. It's advisable to check with your medical doctor at all times.

18. What Is The Difference Between Post-Absorptive And An Absorptive State?

A post-absorptive state is a metabolic period that occurs when the stomach and intestines are empty. During a post-absorptive state, the body's energy needs are fulfilled from energy previously stored in the body. This state is typically reached six or more hours after the food has been consumed, usually overnight, and in the morning before breakfast. A post-absorptive state greatly differs from an absorptive state. An absorptive state occurs during the period within four hours of food consumption. After we consume and digest a meal, glucose and amino acids are transported from the intestines to the blood.

The 'fed' condition leads to the secretion of insulin, which is one of the two most important regulators of fuel metabolism, the other regulator being glucagon. The secretion of the hormone insulin by the pancreas is stimulated by glucose. In essence, insulin signals the fed state and stimulates the storage of fuels and synthesis of proteins in a variety of ways. The liver helps to limit the amount of glucose in the blood during times of plenty by storing it as glycogen in order to be able to release glucose in times of less food.

The high insulin level in the fed state also promotes the entry of glucose into muscles and adipose tissue. Insulin stimulates the synthesis of glycogen by muscle as well as by the liver. During the absorptive state the stomach and intestines contain nutrients that are normally used to meet immediate energy needs of the body. When the body is in an absorptive state, glucose is readily available to be synthesized into energy. During the early fasting state, the blood glucose levels begin to drop leading to a decrease in insulin secretion and a rise in glucagon secretion. Just as insulin signals the fed state, glucagon signals the fasted state. Both muscles and the liver use fatty acids as fuel when the blood glucose level drops. Once the nutrients in the stomach and intestines are exhausted, the body returns to a post-absorptive state during which energy needs are met by stored fuels contained in the body tissues. Once a post-absorptive state is reached, the body begins converting fat to glucose. It is said that a typical well-nourished 70kg man has fuel reserves totaling about 161,000kcal (670,000kj) whereas the energy needed for a twenty-four-hour period ranges from 1,600kcal (6,700kj) to 6,000 kcal (25,000kj), depending on the extent of the individual activity levels. With this analysis, the stored fuel should be sufficient to meet caloric needs in starvation mode for one to three months. However, the carbohydrate reserves are normally depleted within a day. As the blood glucose drops, the rate at which the body secretes insulin slows and the pancreas will then begin to secrete glucagon.

During this journey of IF, I basically preferred short-term fasts for not more than forty-eight hours. With this short-term fast we are basically targeting lipolysis. The free fatty acids are made available by the action of glucagon. In the presence of low insulin levels, glucagon activates an enzyme in adipose cells called hormone sensitive lipase. This enzyme catalyzes the hydrolysis of stored triglycerides and the release of free fatty acids and glycerol into the blood. Glucagon also activates enzymes in the liver that convert some of these fatty acids into ketone bodies which are secreted into the blood. Several organs in the body can use ketone bodies as well as fatty acids. Through the stimulation of lipolysis or fat breakdown and ketogenesis and the formation of ketone bodies, the high glucagon and low insulin levels that occur during fasting provide circulating energy for use in the muscles, liver and other organs. The body hormonal changes help provide adequate levels of blood glucose to sustain the metabolism to the brain. The action of insulin and glucagon promote appropriate metabolic responses during periods of fasting and periods of absorption.

19. What About Electrolyte Loss When Fasting?

Studies have shown that when insulin levels reduce, a person retains less water and possibly loses electrolytes along the way. It will take some time for you to feel dizzy from fasting, but if it does happen it could be an indication that your electrolytes are low. A pinch of sea salt in water or directly on the tongue should improve the situation. Unlike table salt, which contains dextrose (sugar), sea salt contains potassium, iodine, magnesium and other important minerals that our bodies need for survival. I take some electrolyte supplements twice or three times a week to avoid any imbalance but this is because I work out frequently.

20. Will Fasting Make Me Store Fat?

No. Regular eating and snacking every two to three hours from the time you wake up until the time you go to bed will result in suppressing your body's ability to burn fat, thus suppressing fat oxidation. Throughout this eating, the body will always be relying on the food you are eating for energy instead of tapping on the stored energy or stored fat. The inability to access the stored fat will make it difficult to lose this fat. Allowing your body to stay without food lowers your body's insulin and with lower insulin, fat metabolism or lipolysis occurs. Lipolysis is basically a process where your body's stored fat is broken down for energy. All in all, your body burns fat when fasting.

21. Will Fasting Make My Body Enter Into Starvation Mode?

No, your body will not enter into starvation mode, neither will your metabolism slow down if you fast, provided you have extra stored fat. It does not make sense to associate starvation with skipping breakfast or not eating for twenty hours, or even for two days when one's body has excess fat to supply one with energy for the fasting period. According to a 1987 study by Nair et al. in the *American Journal of Clinical Nutrition*, the earliest evidence of a lowered metabolic rate in response to fasting is said to have occurred after sixty hours with an eight per cent drop in resting metabolic rate. A 1994 study published in the *British Journal of Nutrition* reported no change in metabolic rate among twenty-nine men and women who fasted for three days (seventy-two hours). Another 2004 study published in *Obesity Research* studied the metabolic effects on women who ate half the amount of their baseline calories over a three-day period, and still there was no change in their metabolic rate. A 2005 study published in the *American Journal of Clinical Nutrition* on the effects of alternate-day fasting on the metabolic rates among males and females showed no change in metabolic rate. A 2007 study on ten lean males showed that undergoing a three-day fast resulted in no changes in metabolism. Keep in mind that the longest I have fasted for and still got results has been seventy-two hours on a very few occasions. My overall average fasting period is twenty/twenty-two hours and bear in mind that most fasting times happen during our sleep. Furthermore, a 2000 study by Zuaner et al. in the *American Journal of Clinical Nutrition* showed that resting energy expenditure actually increases in early starvation (up to sixty hours) and is accompanied by an increase in plasma norepinephrine. Norepinephrine is a catecholamine in the body that plays a role in the 'fight-or- flight' response, something our ancestors would have relied upon when hunting for food. When the fight-or-fight hormones are released into the bloodstream, they trigger the release of glucose from energy stores and increase fat burning, by releasing fatty acids from your stored fat. This is how your body maintains your blood sugar levels and increases your fuel supply. Starvation could possibly occur if one has little to no excess body fat.

22. If I Don't Eat Every Two To Three Hours, Will It Not Negatively Affect My Blood Sugar Which Will Result In Me Getting Too Hungry Or Even Fainting?

It is interesting that most people believe that they will be shaky, feel light-headed and even faint when they don't eat or simply skip meals, or if they engage in a fasted workout. Always remember that as long as you are not underweight and as long as you are carrying stored fat, then you have enough stored energy to carry you through. Keep well-hydrated and incorporate nutritious meals during your open window. That is how our bodies were designed, to store excess energy and to retrieve it in time of low or no food consumption. One can believe that those imagined symptoms could merely be ingrained anxiety over not eating. It is not possible for a sixteen- or twenty-four-hour period of not eating to place anyone in a state of hypoglycemia. Our bodies were designed to survive during times of food scarcity and therefore it is logical to also conclude that our bodies are designed to be efficient in regulating sugar if we are healthy. The societal norm of eating as soon as we wake up makes the idea of skipping breakfast or any other meal unthinkable and just the thought of skipping breakfast makes a person think of how hungry they will be later on. On the contrary, eating every two to three hours actually results in making you hungrier. That is the reason why once you start to eat you find it difficult to stop. Having a constant regular supply of food trains the body to rely solely on consumed food for energy. The body is never given a break to use the alternative source of energy, i.e. stored fat. The body becomes inefficient in converting fat to energy due to the constantly raised insulin which in turn promotes more fat storage and the development of resistance to insulin. An immediate drop in sugar levels after consuming these regular meals results in more hunger pangs and the circle goes on. In other words, your body never finds the need to tap into your stored glycogen or fat for energy because you are constantly eating and giving the body an immediate energy source. This is one of the reasons why eating carbohydrates every few hours makes you hungry for more carbohydrates every few hours. IF, on the other hand, effectively suppresses your hunger pangs since your insulin is either under control or low, thus enabling fat metabolism. Waiting a few hours for your first meal allows you the opportunity to enjoy your meal when you decide to eat or 'break the fast' to your satisfaction. Always bear in mind that there is always enough glycogen stored in your liver to meet your immediate energy needs, but when the glycogen store gets depleted, your body turns to the stored energy for fuel.

23. How Do I Manage A Plateau? What If I Stop Losing Fat Or Weight?

a) Check your meals. It's possible to go to extremes and forget that whole healthy food should take precedence over occasional treats. So include more unprocessed food during your open window, e.g. fruit, vegetables, lean meat and lots of water.

b) Check your sleep. It's important. Get enough sleep and do your best to keep it from being broken or restless. Treat sleep like an important part of your life, not just the period of time where you 'crashed'. Embrace a night-time routine, respect your sleep time. It's important to have six to eight hours of uninterrupted sleep.

c) Check your gut health. Your gut bacteria play an important role in your ability to lose weight. My thirty years of yo-yo dieting might have done significant damage to my gut. I therefore began adding food that promotes a healthy gut into my daily routine, such as:

- apple cider vinegar (two tablespoons in a cup of warm water just before opening my window)
- plain yoghurt
- fresh fruit and vegetables
- coconut oil
- salmon
- garlic

d) Patience. Let's face it, sometimes there's nothing you can do. Sometimes you've tried everything and nothing works. Sometimes your body just needs time to adjust. You have to be patient and trust the process. You didn't go to bed one night a size 10 and wake up the next morning a size 16. It happened over time. It was gradual. And it's going to take time to get it fixed. So please be patient.

24. What If I Eat Before My Window Opens?

This is not a life sentence but rather a flexible lifestyle. IF = Freedom. Every day is a new day. When you encounter days where you cannot make it to your goal and you eat early, its fine, eat. Then start again. It is that simple. Just keep on taking those little steps that get you to your goal.

25. What Can I Eat During Fasting?

I experience better results when I fast clean. I eat nothing and drink only unsweetened beverages such coffee, tea and water during my fasting times. No juice, no milk and no alcohol during my closed window.

26. I Am Afraid Fasting Will Make Me Hungry

Well, as you will experience, fasting will greatly suppress your hunger. Remember that most of your fast happens when you are sleeping at night. Contrary to what people might think, during the early phases of fasting you will experience low levels of hunger. In most cases people confuse thirst with hunger since both hunger and thirst are controlled by the hypothalamus. It is important to keep well-hydrated, always having a glass of water first whenever feeling any hunger pangs. You can drink

173

as much calorie-free liquid as you want during your closed window.

27. Is It Okay For Me To Fast Anytime?

Yes. However, it important to discuss this with your medical doctor, especially if you have any medical conditions, to obtain consent and ascertain if fasting would be right for your health status.

28. Can I Add A Splash Of Cream Or Milk Or Lemon To My Coffee Or Water?

Yes and no. Different people will respond differently to any addition of a splash of cream or milk to your coffee. It might be ideal to do self-experimentation to see what works for you as an individual. All in all, fasting works because it keeps your insulin levels low enough to allow fat burning or oxidation to occur. Bear in mind that anything that will raise insulin will break the fast.

29. Is 'Bulletproof Coffee' Okay To Consume When Fasting?

I do not consume coconut oil or butter in my fasted state. I am not a fan of adding coconut oil or butter to my morning coffee, and this is why. Although fats have no effect on insulin, consuming these extra calories are not without consequence. Furthermore, research suggests 'bulletproof coffee' may be boosting hyperlipidemia in otherwise healthy individuals. Consult with your physician.

30. How Much Weight Will I Lose In The First Few Weeks?

Weight loss is different from one person to another.

31. What Should I Eat During My (Open Window) Feasting Time?

Just Eat. Eat to nourish your body and remember that treats should be enjoyed in moderation. Your health and fitness goals will also influence your food choices. My choice is mainly 80 per cent non-processed and 20 per cent processed food.

32. What Should I Eat When I Break My Fast?

I have found through experience that coming out of a fast can be tricky. The digestive system is asleep and has to be woken up slowly. You should probably avoid overeating to compensate for the fast as it can lead to nausea, stomach cramps, diarrhea and poor digestion and could ruin the health effects of a good fast. If you want to come out of a fast without gaining weight and shocking your system, you must ease yourself back into a proper eating regimen. Here are a few examples:

- Eat small amounts of raw fruit or vegetables at a time. This will allow your digestive system to wake up slowly and naturally.
- Eat when you are hungry, not according to the clock. Don't continue eating when you are full. Let your body adjust on its own. Avoid overloading your system or else you will feel bloated.
- If you do fast again then try to break the fast in a healthier manner.
- Drink lots of water. Warm water mixed with a little lemon juice will help re-open the stomach and increase its ability to process foods.

33. How Should I Respond To Other People When Offered Food During My Closed Window?

It's always great to live a free life and be open about what you are doing. However, if you feel that you don't have time for lengthy explanations, here are some responses which you might find useful:

- "Thank you, I will eat later"
- "I only eat at specific times"

- "It's not yet my time to eat"
- "Thank you, I have just had a meal"
- "I am on a deferred-time eating schedule"
- "I have just had something to eat, and now I am giving my body a break"

34. How Do I Handle Regular Headaches?

I experienced mild headaches during my first week of fasting. I find that drinking more water throughout the day works for me. Since we also get a lot of water from food, if you delay eating then you are, of course, reducing your intake of water. I also ensured that I occasionally drink electrolytes during my open window.

35. What Can I Add To My Tea Or Coffee For Optimum Results During Fasting?

Nothing. For maximum benefits I preferred clean fasts. Plain water or sparkling water. Plain coffee or tea with no sugar, no honey, no milk.

36. Having Reached My Target Goal, Can I Go Back To My Former Eating Habits?

The fact that you are not your ideal weight now is an indication that your previous way of eating did not serve you well and if you consider going back to it, you can expect the same results. Since it previously resulted in added excess fat, you can be sure that it will do so again. You cannot start a weight-loss lifestyle and expect to go back to your former eating habits without the weight coming right back. To avoid regaining the weight, you have to make this a permanent lifestyle change.

37. If Am Losing Centimeters But Not Weight, Is It Still Fat Loss?

The simple answer is yes, you are losing fat, because you are getting smaller. How is it possible for your body to hold onto weight and still manage to get smaller while you are fasting? Losing centimeters but not weight? You have been fasting for some time, you notice that your clothes fit better, your skin is glowing, and you have more energy, and as far as you are concerned all is perfect. You are still losing fat. But then you step on that 'not so good friend', the scales, and immediately you feel betrayed. This 'not so good friend' insists that you have done nothing. It even states that you have been bad since you have gained weight. Does this sound familiar? What has really happened? It is important not to place your entire trust on what you see on the bathroom scales. Always remember that your body has been saving fat as long as you are overweight. Your body has kept the fat distributed throughout your body. When you start losing fat, it does not trust you to continue whatever path you have chosen that is causing that fat loss. So, when the fat comes off the fat pockets, it injects water as a 'place holder'. Sometimes, water actually replaces the weight of the fat loss or sometimes it replaces the volume. Since water weighs more than fat, when the body replaces fat with water, your weight is likely to stay the same although you might look a bit smaller. Eventually, the body decides that you are not going to replace the fat you have lost, and so it lets go of the water. Thus, when the body fat cells accept that they are no longer needed, the water will be expelled and fat cells will shrink. This is known as the 'Whoosh'. You must have noticed that it is important to drink water during your fasting period and after. Loss of fat is related to water intake.

38. Which If Style Should I Adopt?

Each of the IF protocols are excellent tools for weight loss as for well as maintaining an overall healthy lifestyle. You should be sure to try them out and work out which one will work best for you since we are all different. There are also some other less popular methods of IF, such as spontaneous meal skipping and alternate day fasting, both of which are fairly self-explanatory. Remember, IF is not a miracle diet, it is an eating schedule. You need to ensure you have your meals correct and your fitness right if you want to reach your goals.

39. What Is The Simplest Way To Start?

Tomorrow, make lunch your first meal. If you stop eating at 8pm and don't eat until noon the next day, that's sixteen hours of fasting – perfect for stimulating growth hormone, which boosts metabolism, builds muscle and slows aging. The fact that you sleep through the majority of your fast makes it relatively painless. If you've trained your body to expect food every two hours, then you might feel hungry the first few times when you try fasting. But it will all be in your head. As you get used to using your fat stores for energy, you can push your first meal further back to increase your fasting time. My most preferred protocol is 20:4, fasting for twenty hours and feasting for four hours. I simply stop eating at 9pm and then have my first meal any time after 5pm the following day.

40. Should I Count Calories And Measure My Food?

There's nothing to count and nothing to measure. There are no tables to remember, no special recipes and there is no food to avoid. However, remember to eat to nourish your body.

41. Is Fasting For Sixteen/Twenty-Four /Thirty-Six Hours Difficult?

It's all in your mind. I honestly did not find it hard once I got used to it. I do not mean to make light of it for you. Your first days of fasting will certainly bring a certain degree of discomfort. You will be a little hungry. This is normal and it is nothing to worry about. The longer your fast and the more you practice the habit of fasting, the less hungry you will feel. The reason for this is a hormone called ghrelin that controls hunger. The production of ghrelin is dependent on when you eat. Producing ghrelin makes you want to eat and eating produces ghrelin which makes you want to eat more. All of which explains why most people don't always feel hungry. Fasting will be hard in the beginning, because you've conditioned your body to produce ghrelin on a schedule, and so you have to push through that hunger. However, ghrelin secretion begins to adapt to new eating patterns pretty quickly. Fasting helps you influence this because you're eating less often, which means you will get hungry less often.

42. Isn't Fasting Bad For My Metabolism?

Fasting did not negatively affect my metabolism especially since I was fasting for a short time. The idea that not eating will *slow* your metabolic rate is based on the fact that eating increases your metabolic rate; the increase occurs when you eat due to something called the *Thermic Effect of Feeding* (TEF). Basically, you expend energy to breakdown, digest, absorb and utilize the food you eat. This part is true. What is not true is the suggestion that the more often you eat, the more likely it is that your metabolism will increase, and therefore not eating often can lead to metabolic slowdown.

You may have been conditioned to think that eating five to six small meals per day helps you keep your metabolism elevated. Again, not true. The fact is that TEF is determined by your total energy intake, *not* how often you eat. So, it doesn't matter if you have two meals or eight, as long as you're getting the same number of calories, the effect will be the same. All of which is to say that a daily fast of, let's say, sixteen or twenty-four hours, does not decrease your metabolism.

43. Will Fasting Make Me Store Fat?

No. If you keep eating meals every two to three hours from the time you wake up until the time you go to bed, you will be chronically suppressing fat oxidation (i.e. fat burning). You will never give your body a chance to burn anything other than the food you are eating. You will have a hard time losing fat. Fasting decreases your insulin levels. This is good because lipolysis (the process whereby your stored fat is broken down for energy) will finally be able to occur. Key points: You burn fat when you are fasting. You burn food when you are eating.

44. Isn't It Unhealthy To Skip Breakfast?

No. If you make sure to eat healthy food for the rest of the day, it is fine.

45. Can I Take Supplements While Fasting?

Yes. However, keep in mind that some supplements (like fat-soluble vitamins) may work better when taken with meals.

Chapter 11

My Twelve-Month Intermittent Fasting Journal And Summary Of Key Points

Since this book is basically based on my study of one, I have found it necessary to share my feelings, emotions and experiences month-by-month to help those that might find themselves going through a similar experience. At the very least I hope it will help you see that you are not alone.

When it comes to weight loss, you cannot underestimate the importance of support structures.

I have always had fitness support groups and after discovering this lifestyle I created a Facebook group called 'Planned Eating – Intermittent Fasting Lifestyle' (now renamed 'Just Eat – Intermittent Fasting Lifestyle') for anyone who wants to learn more and get support when pursuing this way of eating.

I also used that platform to coach and assist anyone who needed my help. In addition to the Facebook support group, there was also a small WhatsApp group of ladies I was coaching this lifestyle. You will read the success stories of these people in Chapter 12.

My Intermittent Fasting Diary:

March 2017

- An associate from MyFitnessPal recommends that I should try IF after once again finding my weight loss stalling, as had happened with every previous regime I had tried. I love researching different ideas and methods, so was intrigued to find out about IF.
- I am researching and reading everything and anything on IF. I am so curious about this lifestyle, so I am watching many videos, looking and searching for scientific evidence and success stories. I must admit, though, that I am finding the apparent simplicity of this lifestyle too good to be true.
- I have discovered interesting books from different authors, including:

  - *The Fast-5 Diet* and *AC: the Power of Appetite Correction*, both by Bert Herring;
  - *Delay Don't Deny* by Gin Stephens;
  - *The Complete Guide to Fasting* by Jason Fung, MD with Jimmy Moore;
  - *The Obesity Code: Unlocking the Secrets of Weight Loss* by Jason Fung, MD;

- *The 8-Hour Diet* by David Zinczenko with Peter Moore, among many others.

- I am experiencing mixed feelings. I just cannot believe how my approach to weight loss had been so wrong. Instead of controlling my insulin, my previous approach to weight loss has made my body insulin resistant. However, I feel like I may have finally discovered the key to my long-term health improvement.

- What makes more sense is my discovery of the relationship between insulin and fat burn. It brings to light the reasons why I have been struggling with weight/fat loss even though I was exercising regularly, eating healthily and managing my calories.

- I realize that because of my regular snacking, even on healthy snacks, I have basically become insulin resistant, hence making it difficult to access or burn my stored fat for energy.

- Through my detailed research I realize and appreciate some of the following basic facts about my life to this point:

a) My previous dieting interventions made me gain weight and that was the reason why I did not have any sustainable weight loss and always got stuck on the yo-yo dieting roller coaster.

b) Regular snacking and eating was actually making me hungrier, hence regular snacking had become a normal way of life.

c) Increasing the number of my meals did not necessarily boost my metabolism as was always claimed. My weight and body fat still remained the same and sometimes my body fat even increased due to these frequent meals. I realize that frequent snacking was the cause of my increased appetite. Carrying so-called 'healthy' snacks to nibble on every two to three hours did not prove to be helpful either as these snacks simply kept my insulin high and therefore resulted in zero fat burn.

d) I understand that the reason why I was overweight was because I was rarely giving my body the opportunity to tap into the stored energy due to high insulin levels.

e) It becomes evident that I need to develop a balanced view to exercising and eating at the right time. Exercise should neither be too much nor too little, but rather, my exercise routine should be sustainable. My ten to twelve hours per week was not proving to be either enjoyable or sustainable. Our body, mind and soul need exercise to keep us healthy, happy and alive. On the other hand, the timing of re-fueling the body is also critical.

The reason why most people still gain weight despite exercising regularly is that it is always easy to 'over eat the workout'. *Just because a person has burnt calories through exercising this is not a pass to over compensate with eating anything at any time.*

f) The fact that something is healthy doesn't mean that it can be eaten anytime; meal timing is key. I needed to know when to eat and when to stop.

g) Instead of always obsessing over calories in and calories out, I need to concern myself with meal timing, thus, I need to concern myself with eating within a reasonable time and then give my body sufficient time to use the energy from my last meal.

h) I understand that when we remain for some time without food we also burn off the excess cellular waste that has developed within our bodies and that process is called cellular cleansing (autophagy).

That buildup of waste comes about as a result of consuming excess calories which our bodies did not use entirely. The understanding is that, if we keep eating and snacking when there is no demand for energy, the body will ultimately store up fat and toxic materials within our cells will build up. I came to understand that there has been a growing field of evidence which suggests that fasting may be beneficial in the reduction of certain types of illnesses. Epilepsy in children was controlled by fasting in the past and is still used in some cases today. By giving the brain a steady supply of ketones the brain is much better equipped to regulate itself.

- I appreciate the fact that, for me to burn fat, I should lower my insulin levels to allow the fat-burning hormones to start working. Regardless of all this, I could still not reach my goal weight nor my goal body size.
- An example of my previous calorie-controlled life:

  - **4:30am:** Pre-workout snack or shake.
  - **5am:** Gym time.
  - **7am:** Post-workout protein shake and protein rich breakfast with toast.
  - **11am:** Mid-morning snack (fruit or yoghurt).

- **1pm:** Lunch (mainly a salad with a protein).
- **4pm:** Mid-afternoon snack (protein bar or fruit or nuts or protein shake).
- **7pm:** Dinner (protein with vegetables and a salad and carbohydrates).

I tracked everything I ate and recorded it in MyFitnessPal, and was mostly on point for weight loss. However, no significant sustainable loss was experienced.

- My weight always ranged between 91kg/200lbs and 95kg/209lbs.

April 2017

- I am feeling very excited and optimistic and I make a decision to try IF.
- I want something sustainable and lasting.
- I decide to start off by tracking my fasting times using an application on my phone.
- I decide to stop eating (close my window) daily at 9pm.
- My first meal (opened my window) will be eaten at 1pm the following day. This is known as a 16:8 IF, with two meals a day (lunch and dinner) protocol.
- 1pm is my preferred 'break-fast' time. I have

my normal lunch between 1pm and 2pm and then my dinner between 7pm and 8pm.

- As for dinner meals, I just eat whatever I have prepared for my family and then close the window at 9pm.
- I check my weight once a week, on Fridays, and discover that I am, on average, losing 1.5kg/3.3lbs per week.
- I eat normal meals during my open window. I do not count calories nor do I weigh any food; I eat until satisfied.
- It is the end of my first month practicing IF, and I have lost a total of 5kg/11lbs. My current weight is 88kg/194lbs.

May 2017

- My clothes are feeling loose and I feel lighter.
- People around me are interested in knowing what I am doing differently.
- I create a WhatsApp group with my fitness friends to share my latest discovery. At first some were a bit reluctant to try this lifestyle. However, when they saw my results they became more open-minded and decided to try out this way of eating. (Some of their success stories are in Chapter 12).
- I am inundated with enquiries about this way

of eating. Some people were even sending friendship requests to my personal Facebook page. (Unfortunately, I have long stopped accepting new friends on my personal facebook page).

- I then decide to open a Facebook support group on this new way of eating, 'Planned Eating – Intermittent Fasting Lifestyle'. I direct anyone who enquires about my weight loss to that Facebook page through which I answer questions and share my experiences.

- I share my self-experimentation discovery and experiences on that Facebook page. I also share articles and research, videos and this diary. In less than three months, there were already 300 members from all over the world. (As at January 2018, there were more than 2,500 members).

- I am finding it interesting experimenting with different eating protocols. I initially started with 16:8, then moved on to 18:6. I then realized that I was no longer feeling hungry even after eighteen hours so I moved to 20:4. The 20:4 was my sweet spot until I felt more comfortable with 22:2. I realize that most of the time, a two-hour open window is all I need during the week. Therefore, I have been experimenting with both a 22:2 and a twenty-four-hour fast at least twice a week. I feel comfortable having my first meal any time after 5pm mid-week. By saying after 5pm, I am not referring to forcing myself to eat because it is 5pm – listening to what my body tells me is always key. This is something that most people don't understand. People have a habit of eating just because there is food without necessarily listening to their bodies as to whether they are hungry or not.

- I usually open my window with a light unprocessed snack. Something like fruit or avocado and cucumber salad, or cherry tomatoes and olives, or roasted peanuts. Thereafter I eat dinner with the family after 7pm.

  - When it comes to weekends, I open my window anytime between 1pm and 2pm. Weekends and holidays are my 'flexi-time' days. On these days, a fourteen- to sixteen-hour fasting time is sufficient for me.
  - I feel mostly comfortable with my 22:2, one meal a day protocol (OMAD). I stop eating at 8pm or 9pm and start eating any time after 5pm the following day. This gives me a minimum fasting time of twenty-two hours and an eating time of two hours.
  - I'm now at the end of the second month of IF. I have lost another 6kg/13lbs, bringing

my total weight loss to 11kg/24lbs. My new weight is 82kg/180lbs.

June 2017

- The journey is becoming more exciting, I love the transformation and my new lighter self.
- My sight has improved. I do not need to use my reading glasses all the time.
- The inflammation in my knees and toes seems to be vanishing thanks to autophagy.
- My clothes are getting even looser. I have moved two sizes down from size 16 to size 12.
- My former 'small clothes' closet is now full of 'big clothes'.
- I decide to start the alterations process of my big clothes since everything seems to be too big. It looks like the fat is successfully melting away. My body is efficiently turning to the stored fat for energy.
- I am enjoying my six-hour weekly workouts in a fasted state and still have an overwhelming amount of energy, thanks to fat adaptation.
- My cravings for sweet things are slowly going away; I find myself craving real, non-processed food like avocado and fruit etc.
- Though my tummy always starts grumbling exactly twelve hours after my last meal,

between 8am and 9am, I usually take it as an indication that my glycogen stores are depleted so the tummy is saying "eat more food". I then respond by saying, "It's time to turn to the stored fat bank account for energy." Water has become my best friend.

- I know how to differentiate between physical hunger and emotional hunger. Appetite correction has also kicked in.

- I'm thinking about writing a book about IF. I think I'll call it "Just Eat" as suggested by my daughter. I want to share with others who might be struggling with weight issues. What I am experiencing is too good and I want to share this effortless weight-loss story. I feel that people have the right to appreciate how easy it is to eat anything you want and lose weight. Losing weight with zero cost. No shakes, no slimming pills, no weighing food, simply **JUST EAT** and then Fast.

- It's the end of the third month and I have lost another 5kg/11lbs, bringing my total weight loss in three months to 16kg/35lbs. My new weight is 77kg/169lbs.

July 2017

- My workouts are more enjoyable and fun. I feel very light and more energetic. I exercise because I love to, not because I have to.
- I have a better understanding of my body in terms of what it requires and what it does not need.
- I am experiencing more clarity of mind and feel more inner calm.
- I am, however, experiencing more cold chills than ever before. I learnt that it is due to absence of the heat normally generated during the digestion process.
- My mind is not catching up with the new look. Though I feel light and my clothes are giving evidence to that, at times when I look in a mirror I see the former big self. I think my mind is not catching up with this body transformation so I decide to embrace and enjoy the new me.
- I am getting both positive and negative feedback. On the one hand, my family and friends are so impressed and very excited for my new look, whilst on the other hand people tell me I am too thin and look sick, and should stop whatever I am doing.

- My view is that, "those who mind don't matter; those who matter don't mind" and, "I am a priority and everything else is an option".
- I now appreciate more food flavors, aromas and textures. Surprisingly, I am starting to be curious and decide to reconcile with my long-lost favorite – chocolate. So I decide to have my favorite chocolate as a treat once or twice a week. However, during this particular week, this became a daily treat.
- Since dinner has now become my only meal, I carefully plan our family dinners to be special feasting occasions with a variety of foods and including a dessert.
- I am also fully reconciled with another of my old favorites, which had been forbidden during my dieting days: my homemade rolls with butter.
- Life is easy and less expensive. No snacks to take to work; water and electrolytes is all that I need.
- My kids are very excited with this way of eating since we can all enjoy our pizza dates as a family without mummy fussing about calories.
- My husband who has also been randomly eating two meals a day, has also dropped a size from L to M.
- The end of the month, and my new sizes are 8/10.

- Though my body is still shrinking, the scale is no longer moving faster like previous months. My weight has still remained at 77kg/169lbs.

August 2017

- It has now been four months since I embarked on this lifestyle. I feel I am starting to feel too comfortable. Sometimes I extend my open window longer than necessary. This stage is normally referred to as 'a teenage rebellious stage'. My special occasional reconciliations with my old favorite treats are becoming a habit. It's true, old habits die hard.
- I decide it's time to tighten things up once more and stick to my set routine in order to get into a 'Do It' stage. Therefore, instead of having treats every day, I resolved to limiting those to once or twice a week.
- I decide to draw up my simple eating plan routine as follows as a guide:

My Flexible Eating Plan

Mon, Wed and Thurs	Eat any time after 7:30pm
Tues	Eat any time after 8:30pm
Fri	Eat any time after 5pm
Sat and Sun	Eat any time after 1pm

I normally stop eating by 8pm or 9pm at the latest.

- I derive motivation from my before-and-after monthly progress picture. I share these monthly progress comparative pictures on my Planned Eating IF Lifestyle Facebook page. This strategy worked positively on my self-motivation especially since my weight loss had plateaued.
- My family and friends are very complimentary. As for my husband, he is my regular photographer.
- I enjoy daily discoveries on this way of eating and I also share some of these discoveries on my Facebook page.
- Ever since I started this way of eating, the relationship between my body and my brain has grown stronger. We communicate much better and our listening skills have greatly

improved. I have learnt to effectively listen to my body and in turn my body listens to me. I listen and comply when my body does not want to be stuffed with food or things it doesn't want and immediately stop. On the other hand, my body listens to me when I remind it to feed from my stored fat for energy when my window is closed.

- Here's an interesting conversation I had with my sister (who is slim): she notices my new slim self and asks me what I changed. I say, "I now eat only once a day." She then asks, "How many times were you eating before?" She then goes on to say that, whenever she decides to eat more than once a day, she gets funny stomach cramps. So for all her life she has been eating one light snack and one main meal. This made me regret all the torture and stress I had been exposing my body to all these years with so many meals and snacks.

- This is what happened at a lunch gathering with a few friends this afternoon.

- Someone asked me if was going to eat and I said I just had something before I left home. And then the other person asked me what I usually eat. They were all surprised when I said I eat anything that my family is eating. Sounding surprised, they encouraged me to continue with what I was doing since it was working.

- After eating all their lunch and desserts, another person said, "Oh I am so full and tired. I wish I could have a nap." I thought to myself, "That's because excess food makes you tired."

- I appreciate that fasting requires an element of self-discipline. Most of us are conditioned both psychologically and hormonally to eat multiple times during the day, and any deviation from this causes people to get cranky. *This is not healthy*. Fasting also requires us to be present with the initial discomfort of not stuffing our faces every time we feel like it. This is a reversal of the typical power structure in body-brain relations. It puts us in the position of consciously making the decision to eat or not to eat, rather than our stomach (aka hormones) effectively making that decision for us. Almost all of us would benefit hugely from consciously redefining our relationship with food, and fasting is an opportunity to do just that.

- It's Friday morning and I just became curious about how much I weigh, since my clothes were feeling very loose. So I decided to hop on my bathroom scales. However, my weight at the end of August is 77kg/169lbs, the same as at the end of July. Though my fat is melting away and I am shrinking, the weight is still consistent. Well, I guess I should give my body time to readjust. Moving from 93kg/205lbs to 77kg/169bs is a big deal and I am sure my body is still adjusting and recalibrating.

- I make a decision to take a three-month break from the scale and only focus on non-scale victories such as fitting in smaller clothes, having increased energy and feeling good.

September, October and November 2017

- I feel so great with zero pressure to weigh myself. My life is now getting so natural.
- My shoes are all too big. It seems like my feet have also shrunk. My shoe size is now 7/8, down from size 8/9.
- My life is no longer controlled by numbers of an arbitrary target. However, I think I am still getting smaller because my gym clothes are way too big. I thought I could delay my gym wear shopping, but it looks like I should replace a few things quickly. Therefore, I decided to go to the sportswear shop. I am not sure which size to try on since I have always been an XXL/XL. Well, I decide to skip a size L and go on to try a size M. Wow! Not only did M fit me, it was even a bit loose! It made me

realize that I was doing really well and must keep going. It brought to mind a conversation I had with my wonderful coach, Gin Stephens, about goal sizes.

- Gin told me that the body will settle where it was meant to. Ever since the day we had that discussion, I resolved to worry less about goal size but rather listen, relearn and to look forward to the new Rachel.

December 2017, January 2018 And April 2018

- It all feels so natural now. This is my new normal.
- I cannot wait to share my book with the world to liberate those who might still be trapped in the expensive yo-yo diets industry.
- It is so much fun shopping for small-sized clothes and shoes. My daughter and I are enjoying our time together while shopping.
- We went on vacation and I decided to only skip breakfast and have a wide open eating window for the day. I had earned the right to do so and could be flexible.
- When I got back from vacation I decided to check how much weight I had gained. I was surprised to see that I had only gained 5kg/11lbs during the four weeks I have been

away. This weight gain does not bother me much. Normally, before IF lifestyle, I could have gained 10kg/22lbs or more.

- I was not worried since I knew that most of this weight was water weight from the excessive carbohydrates and sugars which I enjoyed during vacation. The fact that my small clothes could fit perfectly, confirmed that it was not fat gain.

- I went back to my fasting protocol of 22:2 OMAD and I decided to do a seventy-two-hour water only, extended fast to self-cleanse and detox. Within five days, the 5kg/11lbs vacation weight and an additional 2kg/4.4lbs had gone.

- *My life is fun. I feel light. My appetite is corrected. I enjoy my exercises in fasted state. I enjoy meals. I am saving money. My body loves the breaks I give it from always focusing on digestion. I eat to live, not live to eat. **I Just Eat.***

Chapter 12

Testimonials Of Others Who Have Succeeded By Using Intermittent Fasting

I have the pleasure of sharing the lives of those that have been impacted on positively by the IF lifestyle. Since I have already given you my pre and post-IF lifestyle, I will only therefore mention my fact profile.

1. Rachel Nekati

- I live in Gaborone, Botswana
- A wife and a loving mother to two beautiful children.
- Management Training and Business Consultant and an Entrepreneur.

Height: 164cm (5'4")
Starting weight: 95kg (209lbs)

Current weight: 70kg (154lbs)
Total lost weight: 25kg (55lbs)
Goal weight: 65kg (143lbs)
Starting size: ....UK 16/18
Current size: ....UK 8/10

Goal size: Where my body decides to settle

2. Dawn Herbert

* Lives in Missouri, United States
* Married for six years and a mother of three, two of whom are adults and one preschooler. I am a stay-at-home mom.

Height: ....164cm (5'4")
Starting weight: 84kg (185lbs)
Current weight: 71kg (157lbs)
Total lost weight: 13kg (29lbs)
Goal weight: 57kg (126lbs)
Starting size: 16/18
Current size: 10/12

Goal size: 8/10 or wherever my body settles

Who Am I?

Dawn Herbert, from Missouri, USA. I'm 46 years of age. I grew up skinny, naturally eating only when I was hungry. My weight started increasing when I was 21. My new husband (at that time) and my dad both told me I was too skinny, so I started eating more. I also moved to a colder climate and became less active. Three months later my new hubby told me I had gained too much weight. This started the emotional eating. I've tried and failed to outrun a bad diet, did low-fat diet, low-calorie diet, South Beach diet, drank Medifast shakes and took Phentermine. I was also on two kinds of injected insulin with my last pregnancy, as I was a gestational diabetic. After this pregnancy, I became a full blown type-2 diabetic, needing 1,500mg of Metformin a day and it barely affected my blood sugar levels. My endocrinologist was telling me I had to lose weight or I'd be back on insulin. I was fatigued, puffy and ached all the time. I felt like a failure as I couldn't get the scale to move down, and it was actually creeping up. I was afraid I was on the verge of my health deteriorating to the point of no return, due to some symptoms I was living with. I was not ready to give up. I just didn't know what to do, and I was running out of energy to try. The love and support of my husband and three kids kept me going, though.

Then, someone whose opinions I respect mentioned IF to me. My first thought, upon reading about it, was that I would be doing harm to my metabolism, and I thought going into starvation mode was a possibility. She told me to read *The Obesity Code* by Dr Jason Fung, and my road to healing began at the age of 45. I will always be grateful to her for saving my life.

Why I Chose Intermittent Fasting

My five-year-old son is autistic, with a very limited list of foods that he will eat. I didn't want to have to make separate meals for us (since I was so exhausted), and I wanted to make sure we could still eat out at a particular restaurant where they give him a toy with his meal. So I decided to try IF.

After a while, I began craving healthy foods for the first time in my life. Now I get irritated if I have to eat low-quality, non-nutritious foods. I'm paying more attention to the ingredients in my food, and trying to make better decisions. I also do not deny myself carbohydrates, or dessert. I am focusing on my gut health, and I don't believe limiting food groups is what I want to do at this point in my life. My health is improving and my blood sugar levels are so much lower now. I will take things day by day and see where my road to health leads me.

The Foods I Eat

I love my salad. Kale/broccoli/cabbage/radicchio with dried cranberries, roasted pumpkin seeds, poppy seed dressing, goats' cheese and a whole avocado. I might add more cranberry trail mix to it as well, as that is another of my new favorite foods. I eat steaks, roasts and hamburger meat. I love roasting my vegetables, and sautéing them in healthy fats. I eat baked and mashed potatoes, and potato salad for the resistant starch. I crave my burritos and pintos and cheese bowl, and this is what I have on days when I just need a fast and easy meal. I love to cook chili, and bean soups. I eat an avocado most days, sometimes with tortilla chips. Quinoa and brown rice have been known to show up on my dinner table. Walnuts, almonds, pecans, pumpkin and sunflower seeds are a great side for me now. Yes, I eat desserts. I eat birthday cake, holiday pies, fun-size candy bars, and maybe a handful of chips or cookies. The quantity is much less than I used to eat. I think if I had to cut out sugar completely it would backfire on me at this point in my life. The longer I fast, the less these foods call out to me and I find I can still eat them while getting healthier. The only things I really limit are pasta, and my husband gets ill when he eats poultry and fish.

I love to cook and I am cooking from all my cookbooks! I got rid of all the 'diet' ones. I eat full fat dairy, no fake sugars, and I try to avoid MSG and processed food filled with chemicals when I can. I am known to have some meatless meals, but cannot see myself eating anything called meat substitute.

I am trying to eat until I am satisfied, and not stuffed. Appetite correction is happening slowly but surely for me. There was a time in my life when my body rebelled and I could not hold down any food, until they put me in the hospital and gave me an IV and medicine. I suffered from hyperemesis gravidarum (HG) with my first pregnancy. I spent a month deteriorating and lost 27lbs before I could get my doctor to do anything. I finally caught his attention when I passed out alone at home. It was a helpless feeling not to be able to eat. I believe that set me up for some binging after I could eat again. It altered my relationship with food. It made me fear hunger.

What Do I Drink During My Fast?

I love my black coffee or tea, with no artificial or natural flavors. This is amazing from someone whose coffee always used to be loaded with creamer. Coffee stimulates autophagy, and decreases my hunger. I also try to drink plain sparkling mineral water once a day. I love the bubbles and nourishing my body with the much-needed minerals. I drink water when I'm thirsty, with no daily goal in mind.

What Do I Drink In My Window?

I have found a brand and flavor of kombucha that I love. I drink freshly squeezed lemon juice in water, and whole milk occasionally. I've also added the creamer to my coffee that I used to love. I threw it away though, as I could really taste the chemicals.

My Non-Scale Victories

These are the things that kept me going, and see this as a lifestyle choice, not a diet. My feet stopped swelling at night. My wedding ring is loose, and twirls all around my finger now. The back pain I would experience in the middle of the night is gone. My face is not as oily as it once was, and my adult acne is reduced to one lone blemish on occasion. My heels aren't as dry and cracked as they once were. My mood is improved, and my depression is gone. That was a huge one, as I was on antidepressants for over ten years.

I just quit taking them because they weren't really helping, and I was tired of the side effects. I am feeling so much better about myself as I have figured out how to get healthier, and I'm not worried about gaining back the weight. I know that, as I fast, I am cleaning up the junky cells in my body that someday could cause sickness or disease. Some days my energy is off the charts, and I used to live in a state of fatigue. My house is cleaner now than it has ever been, and my new hobby is de-cluttering.

I love cooking again. As it's just one meal a day... I want it to be great! I have more time to do what I enjoy. My brain fog is lifted. I can read now and comprehend what it says. Reading used to be overwhelming. I'm back in my pre-pregnancy clothes (well, the small number that I kept). I feel lighter and stronger. Loose and saggy skin is tightening up due to the process of autophagy. I don't feel deprived. I'm craving healthier foods. My fasting blood sugar levels have plummeted. I no longer fear going back on insulin. Plus, I used to be so fatigued during my period week that I would only be able to do the bare minimum and fall back into bed. Now it's just another week in my month – barely noticeable.

My Scale Victories

I was 185lbs when I began fasting thirteen months ago. This morning I weighed in at 158lbs. I probably could have lost more on the scale, but I eat what I

213

want and I don't feel deprived. 27lbs is a victory to me! My body will release the weight when it is ready.

Did I Exercise?

When I first began IF thirteen months ago I was exhausted from trying to outrun a bad diet. I made a conscious decision to not exercise until I was ready. Healing my mind from so many years of searching for a lower number on the scale and failing is really a big deal for me.

I did run my first 5k marathon, with my friends' encouragement. We met at the lake once a week for a couple of months beforehand. I didn't really do anything else to get ready for it. I walked fast/jogged my first 5k in 53:00.

(I did it twelve hours into a fast, and didn't break fast until twenty-two hours in. I was very active that day.) Could I have done that before fasting? I'm not so sure…

I do know that exercise makes me feel good, and improves my health as well. It won't be long until I decide to do it consistently. I will do it because I want to, and not because I have to. I will move because I love how strong and capable I feel. I will move because it helps me feel happy.

My Measurements

In the past thirteen months I have lost the following amounts just from IF: 1" from my neck, 3.5" from my bra band, 4" from my belly, 1.5" from each bicep, 2.5" from each thigh, 3" from my breasts, and 4" from my hips.

Conclusion

My story is not over yet, but I'm pretty happy about where I am today.

3. Debbs

- 29 years old
- Married with one beautiful daughter
- Lives in Gaborone, Botswana

Height: .... 159cm (5'2")
Starting weight: 68kg (150lbs)
Current weight: 58kg (128lbs)
Goal weight: 54kg (119lbs)
Starting size: .... UK 12
Current size: .... UK 8

Goal size: UK 6

Before I started the IF journey, I was miserable in a lot of ways. After having a C-section, I developed a pouch that just wouldn't go away, even though I tried many slimming teas and belts. Nothing worked. I felt stuck and I didn't know why my body could not go back to its original size 6 which I had been throughout my life. My original size has always been UK size 4 and 6 depending on the styles and now I was stuck on UK size 12. With my oval face and being fat, I did not look good in photos.

I had to master the skill of looking at a certain angle so that I can look good in my pictures. The excess weight affected my confidence level greatly.

I will never forget the year 2017. It was the year when my sister-in-law (the author of this life-changing book) introduced me to IF. Little did I know that this lifestyle would change my life forever. I immediately tried this lifestyle on my own for a few weeks and during that time I dropped one size. I moved from size 12 to 10 with ease. I was so excited, though it was not easy since I was doing it on my own as my husband wasn't too keen to join me nor wanted to try clean eating. I found myself becoming more reluctant to stick to my eating times due to the availability of many tempting foods around the house. In January 2018, things changed.

My husband made a decision to try IF – what a blessing! He did his research and was convinced by the scientific evidence of this lifestyle and he fell in love with this way of eating. My husband was highly motivated and determined, more than me!

Doing IF together reminded me of the early days of our relationship, ten years ago. It increased the romantic bond between us and we enjoy discussing what we are going to open our windows with. I am very excited to say I feel good in my size 8 and that the pouch which I had has long since disappeared.

Before embarking on this lifestyle, my husband and I used to make fun of our weight gain ever since we got married and we had reached a point where hugging was very different since there were barriers in between due to our big tummies. Today we both feel young again, happy and more confident since we can easily hug without any barriers. When my husband and I started this journey, our objective was to lose weight and look good for each other, but now it is more than that. We both feel healthy and have easily added exercise to it. This lifestyle increased our intimacy with each other and it feels like we are falling in love again. Our feelings for each other are mutual. When I look at my husband all I see is the sexy man I fell in love with. I feel beautiful and look beautiful with an amazing energy.

We both enjoy this way of eating and are very happy with it. We look forward to continuing with this lifestyle forever. I am so grateful to my sister-in-law for introducing this lifestyle to us. She has given us the best gift anyone could ever give us – a chance to change our lives and live a healthy, fulfilling life which will allow us to enjoy special moments with our beautiful daughter as we watch her grow up. My sister-in-law has empowered us with so much knowledge and we will always cherish it. Our marriage has been revitalized. Thank you once more.

4. Wapa

- 38 years old
- Married
- Three children, two boys and a girl, aged nine, seven and six years, respectively.

Height:	161cm (5'3")
Starting weight:	75kg (165lbs)
Current weight:	Have not weighed myself for some time
Goal weight:	65kg (143lbs)
Starting Size:	UK 14 (38)
Current Size:	UK 12 (36)

Goal Size: UK 10 (34)

Growing up as a 'big' child was never easy. I loved food! And I still do! When it was time to play, I would opt for easy games where running and jumping were not required. I would choose friends of a similar size so we could laze around together. At school, other kids would have their uniforms bought from the shops but mine had to be tailor made. When going shopping for new clothes, my mum would shoot straight to the adult section. We would get adult clothes and have them altered to fit my chubby body.

As I grew up, responsibilities and commitments came. I had less time to eat and no appetite at times as I would be swamped with work. This was when I was now at high school and in tertiary education. At tertiary level it was worse, as there were deadlines to meet and less time for eating. I would only have one meal a day.

I lost weight tremendously and I would admit that I loved it. I gained more confidence. I went shopping with other girls on not so busy days and had the liberty of picking different clothes from different sections in 'normal' sizes and designs like other girls my age. No more hiding the 'meat'! It was time to expose the beauty from within which was also now on the outside. At that time, I never knew that I was practicing IF by default.

I finished my studies, got married and continued with my beautiful 'normal' sized body. I was a size 34 (UK size 10). I loved every bit of it, until I got pregnant! I started eating for two as I would get extremely hungry. My body ballooned in size as all the fat came back. I had my first child, second child and third child with the same 'big' body. I struggled to lose weight afterwards. I was at 81kg (178lbs.). I tried all sorts of diets and exercises, but failed. I would get different illnesses, one after the other: flu, thrush, headache, fatigue, skin rashes, sore throat – the list is endless. It never entered my mind that the reason I had lost weight while studying was because of the way I was eating. I didn't relate any of that to wellness.

In 2015, I met with Rachel and the other ladies at the gym for a boot camp program. We used to see each other at the gym and greet each other and it ended there, until we joined boot camp. It was clear that we were all determined to lose weight. We created a WhatsApp group and started sharing information and eating plans. We tried all sorts of those but didn't actually reach where we wanted to be. In 2016, Rachel suggested we start eating clean. We all started the plan. It kind of worked, but so slowly! I would say Rachel was the leader. She is consistent and would religiously follow or adhere to what she embarked on. I would follow suit as I saw the results she was getting and would also at times chat and discuss other ways of overcoming our problems. I went from size 40 (UK 16) to size 38 (UK 14), 81kg (178lbs) to 75kg (165lbs), and got stuck there.

2017! The year of results! Rachel came across some article, I think, on IF. She told me about it so we gave it a try. I went in fully! I researched IF and gave it a try. There was no difficulty at all. I could eat my favorite food but just had to work on my timing. I got so over excited with IF that I overlooked my low blood pressure issue. I unknowingly had low blood pressure when I was young and it was worsened by childbearing. I only had one meal a day. I would do two twenty-four-hour fasts per week, alternated 20:4 and 22:2 on the other two days and 18:6 for the weekend. It put a smile on my face as I saw the results faster than I ever expected. I went one size down, from size 38 to size 36 within a month. I decided to do away with the scale reading and just enjoyed the Non Scale Victories (NSV). I got carried away and did a forty-two-hour fast, which helped the fat loss but backfired because I didn't take precaution for low blood pressure!

I became weak as time went on. I would feel dizzy and fatigued. I consulted with the doctor, researched and also posted to the group to hear their views. Great advice was given, to slow things down! I decided not to go overboard. I reduced the fasting hours increased my electrolytes intake and started to feel better. I am currently doing 20:4 twice a week, and 18:6 during the other five days. Things only change when I am on my period as I would more iron. So, I do 16:8 on those days. I do at times squeeze in a twenty-four-hour fast once a week when things are good. Right now I am somewhere between a size 36 (UK 12) and a size 34 (UK 10). I know this because size 36 clothes are loose and size 34 fits but can be a bit tight. Some size 34 clothes fit well; I guess it depends on the design and fabric.

The IF time schedule that I am currently on works well for me as I am able to take in the required nutrients for my condition, feast on my favorite food and, as I am also an active person, I am able to do my workouts, mostly cycling (which is my favorite), without feeling weak! There is progress, though slow, but I am grateful! #IFForLife! #Happiness!

5. Susan

- Married
- Children: Biologically two and four adopted

Height: ....165cm (5'5")
Starting Weight: 73kg (161lbs)

Current Weight: 68kg (150lbs)
Goal Weight: 65kg (143lbs)
Starting size: UK 12
Current size: UK 8

Goal size: UK 6

I grew up very skinny until 2004 after giving birth to my second and last child. Before then my maximum weight ever was 55kg. During pregnancy, I gained 28kg and after the birth my weight remained at 73kg. Before pregnancy, my dress size was between UK 6 and 8 (32 and 34). Then, after the birth, I found I was size 12 (36). People did not recognize me except for my facial marks/scars and when I greeted them, they would say, "I saw the resemblance and I was wondering if it's you," and some would ask me what had happened to me. Then I would say I had a new baby. I continued to call myself a new mum for two years. Then one day during a church service, the pastor started telling us how we lose our identity to challenges or situations in our lives, for example when you are sick you are no longer called Susan but a sickly one, or if you lose your spouse you are called a widow, and so on. That hit home for me because that is exactly what I was doing by calling myself, "*motsetsi*" (a new mum). The following week when I got to work I joined the wellness team. That is when I learnt about Nature Care. I was told about the blood group diet and colon cleansing, which I did immediately. I started following the blood group diet. It worked for a few months because I would get relief from bloating and constipation and shed a few kilos, but thereafter I was back to the suffering again. I ended up buying the products and doing it at home. A friend used to say, "Susan this is not right, you are hurting your colon, please find something with a permanent solution." But there was none. Everything I tried was short-lived. At one point I was nicknamed "Detoxification Specialist" because I knew everything about detoxing.

I visited a hydro spa. I became a vegan because the blood group diet said I could not digest meat. (That's a belief I still hold. I am so scared of eating meat because of constipation. I suffered with piles as a result.) My biggest challenge has always been bloating and constipation. The extra fat now accumulated on my midsection and inner thighs. In summer, my thighs rub against each other. Imagine the friction, the heat created that causes real burning like when you are wearing a tight-fitting shoe in summer and you develop blisters. That is the pain, therefore I have to wear tights to avoid them rubbing against each other, and I then discovered Spanx™. All I did only brought temporary relief.

Until my high school friend Rachel introduced me to planned eating, or IF. I started immediately with the 16:8 eating protocol for a month while at the same time I was reading a lot about IF. The second month, I increased to 20:4, then to OMAD which I've been doing since 30 December 2017.

By the way, I started IF on 22 September 2017, weighing (160lbs) 73kg and with a BMI of 28. A week into IF, I started feeling relief from bloating and constipation. I understood the difference between hunger and starvation, because I knew I do not have to throw anything in my mouth each time I feel hungry, I understood that the longer I maintained my fasted state, the more beneficial it is to my body because of autophagy. Then, a month later, I realized I did not feel hungry anymore and, when it was time to open my window, I appreciated food more than ever because my taste buds had changed.

In terms of the bathroom scales, my weight remained the same two months after starting IF, despite the compliments and my feeling lighter, more energetic with glowing skin.

I decided to forget about it and focus on non scale victories until, on 22 January 2018 (that is exactly four months since I started), I realized that I had lost

5kg (11lbs), down to 68kg (149lbs). My goal weight is 65kg (143lbs).

I started at size UK 12 (36), and I am now ranging between size 6 (30) and 8 (32) depending on the cut. In terms of pants I have had to completely change my wardrobe to UK 6 (30). My bra size was 34DD but has now dropped to just one D, and my shoes are too big! But above all I am very happy, I have inner peace, self-esteem is high, confidence is back and I'm getting a six-pack. This has become my permanent lifestyle. #nostopping.

6. Nita

- Lives in California
- Widowed
- Retired

Height: 162.5cm (5'4")
Weight: 51–52kg (112–114lbs)
Starting weight: 60kg (133lbs)

Goal weight: to stay at or under 52kg (114lbs)

Biography

I am 66 years old, and for the first time in my life I am at my dream weight. I never thought it would be possible and had actually cleaned out my closet getting rid of clothing items that I was convinced I would never fit into again. A friend introduced me to IF and it has changed my life!

My Story

I was raised in a very strict, authoritarian home where criticism was the norm. Praise was seldom, if ever, heard. Unbeknownst to me, I did not know that 'fat shaming' (a term that was non-existent at the time) was wrong. Thinking it was perfectly normal to judge people by their appearances and weight, the concept that laziness or ambition had no correlation to weight or self-worth wasn't clear to me until much later into my adult life. I had no idea that I had self-esteem issues.

In the era where Twiggy was the standard and every teenage girl's idol, those of us who did not have the figure of that famous model bought into the idea that we were not good enough. I remember feeling so ashamed that I wasn't tall and thin, dreading going to school and being so envious of those thin girls wearing hip-hugging skirts and clinging sweaters.

I remember my very first diet at the age of 16. It was summer vacation and I was determined to start school in September as a thinner me. So I counted calories, cut out all sweets, and went from 148lbs (67kg) to 125lbs (56kg). But I still felt 'fat' inside. Every time I saw my reflection in the mirror, I would compare myself to tall thin girls and still feel inadequate.

My constant dieting, weight gains and weight losses continued throughout my whole life. The most I ever weighed was 164lbs (74kg) and wore size 16. I remember being so very unhappy and eating to comfort myself. Getting up in the morning and dreading to fit into too tight clothing, being uncomfortable with buttons and zippers poking me is a feeling I would not wish upon anyone. The scale became my enemy, dictating if I was going to have a good day or a bad day! The desperation I felt about my increasing weight was crushing.

I read every article on 'dressing thin'. There wasn't any diet I wasn't willing to try: Weight Watchers (old school before point system), counting calories, Atkins, Cabbage Soup diet, Grapefruit diet, Nutra Systems, Weight Watchers Point system, Mediterranean, South Beach, Black coffee/yoghurt/green apple diet, 1,000 calorie diet, Liquid Protein Diet; you name it, I tried it. I did like the low-carb eating of the South Beach diet. So when I found IF in July of 2017, I combined low-carb eating with OMAD. Then I tried a twenty-four-hour fast, and steadily increased this to forty-eight hours. It was a very hot summer, so my appetite wasn't all that great. Plus my relationship with my boyfriend ended very abruptly, so between the heartbreak and hot weather, I was able to reach my goal weight under eight weeks doing mostly OMAD, eating a low-carb diet and doing Zumba dancing.

In September, I went on a seven-week trip to Holland and Indonesia fearing that I would gain all my weight back. But I was able to indulge myself when I saw something I really wanted to eat. I did not go wild, and was very selective, but a good pastry, coconut ice cream, a beer here and there, or a cocktail were all part of my vacation treats. In Holland, especially, those famous French fries stands they have everywhere permeating the air with that wonderful smell did NOT get passed up.

Confession

I do still struggle with my body image and still cannot believe my eyes when I look in the mirror.

I was recently criticized for being too thin. Instead of being disappointed or angry for not getting the support I was hoping to receive, I celebrated my personal victory and rejoiced in being and feeling thin!

Continuing Journey

IF has opened the door for me to continue my own personal growth and development. I am learning to work on self-acceptance, self-care, self-love, and validating myself without the need for other people's approval. I feel freed from my emotional eating habits, and am learning to accept my feelings and work through them by journaling, meditation and reading uplifting motivational books. IF has changed my relationship with food and it has opened the door for a whole new way of life for me. I feel empowered with the knowledge that I CAN make changes in my life regardless of the naysayers! I do not share IF with many people because, in my family, food is love. Any rejection of food offerings is seen as personal rejection. So I learned to plan my fasting and eating around family visits. My hero is Dr Jason Fung and Dr Mercola on YouTube. I was recently taken off statin drugs for my familial high cholesterol issue because of the side effects my body was experiencing. My next doctor's appointment is four months from now, so it will be challenging to maintain my weight and get my cholesterol down, but I am positive I can do it. I am so excited about my new life and my only regret is that I did not find IF sooner!

7. Wincey

- Married with two children

Starting weight:	85kg
Current weight:	78kg
Goal weight:	60kg
Height:	1.56m
Starting size:	UK 16/18
Current size:	UK 14

Goal size: UK 10

I was born with a healthy chubby face, not skinny nor roll fat, well into adolescence until 17 years of age. Then I joined the fat fight army and I started gaining weight. It started on my last year of senior secondary school, attracting a vicious rumour in school that I might be pregnant. The good side of the rumour though was that it broke me out of my shell of being somehow reserved; I became Nancy Drew the mystery detective, as I incessantly sought who would've started such a rumour.

But a death knell had been dealt to my self-esteem. I started my journey of slimming aids. I got myself some little green tablets that promised to "eat away unwanted fat while I slept" and without changing my normal eating habits. Hahaha... I went onto them with such zest and zeal that though I didn't immediately wake the next day being as thin as Kate Moss, I kept on them and lost quite a bit by month end. I took them for some time until everyone started noticing and I was back to looking good and acceptable. That was to be short-lived, the following years from 1993 to 1995 I gained double the weight which I had initially lost. It didn't immediately make me as self-conscious as I felt when I was at school, more especially that I was on National Service in a rural area far, far-away from home and those who knew me. It also didn't matter much because I had a room-mate who was twice my size and she carried it happily and without a care! And we ended being called Piggy-Porky. It made me slightly uncomfortable until I realised my room-mate was almost relishing the nicknames. She would be dancing like crazy while our friends were laughing and chanting the names, and as it followed, I became part of the circus performance and a respected member of the two dancing little pigs! Until I came back home a whopping 90+kg of lard, my parents have never seen me that big. My father could not hide his shock! He was more concerned about me having a heart attack than aesthetics. I hit the gym, got myself some ephedrine, and other appetite suppressants and meal replacements.

Being active has never been a problem, I played softball at school and I was not that bad. I also adored athletics. I so loved running, I still do. I dreamt of the whole stadium rousing when I was on the track, I dreamt of being a revered track star and during sport season I would try with my whole being to run as fast as I could. In my mind, I would be flying and totally killing at the tail. I would finish feeling so jaded but to a very entertained group of people who saw some round ball bobbing at the tail of the runners!

I have never thought myself as beautiful until now. Of course, I knew I was not deformed or had anything protruding so much out of my face or somewhere in the body, that would make me feel unusually 'ugly', I had an okay face that would occasionally be mistaken for pretty! I knew I had an above-average beautiful smile that seems to get attention. Still such would make me very uncomfortable, because fat isn't beautiful, I can't wear certain cuts of clothing or even afford to wear a tummy baring T-shirt like everyone else my age at that time.

I therefore grew to prefer being in the background; not doing anything to attract attention to how I look. Not talk loud, not dress fashionably. No, nothing! I wanted to BLEND in, something that I grew up with, and I came to realise that it held me back in a lot more aspects of my life, academically and professionally. I didn't do badly and I am not doing that bad as an adult either but I realise I could have been phenomenal if I had been more confident to stand out. And I have a wardrobe with 90 per cent navy blue! Not black or dread brown! Navy made me feel safe, not drab or too sombre but mute yet still cool. I got to navy blue because I believe it is complementary to my skin colour – it brings out my eyes! It worked for me because given that the only part I don't mind appearing on pics would be part of my upper body, not too direct or focused either, just a side glance! That is the other thing, I have hated taking pictures all my life because of how 'fat' I looked and terrible it made me feel. On group selfies, I would strategically hide between others and poke a 'funny' face, just to fit in. and now my kids think good picture moments are when you make faces to the camera/phone!

Most of my clothes are roomy shirts, leggings, cargo pants, relaxed dresses. I dream of a nice shift dress or pant suit but I would rather wear some chinos and a comfortable top, always with a little knit sweater or jacket or SOMETHING to hide the bulk! I am always conscious my arms don't show and my tummy/waist are be hidden.

I remember one time I was at my grandmother's house with a whole lot of kin, preparing for her 100th birthday in 2014. Something possessed me to pose full-on for pictures that day … and lo and behold! I looked like a hippo at a dry hole in the delta! One prick, I could burst into smithereens of pinkish fatty matter for a whole square kilometre! I was filled with such dreadful self-loathing at that moment I went into a drastic diet of green salad dressed with vinegar, until I felt I was going to faint, which rarely happens because I also got into 30mg of Duromine! The pill left me with such a dry mouth, sometimes my mouth would be left lopsided as though I had had a mild stroke. But it was good for me. No eating for at least six weeks and I only lost 12kgs! And I felt so good. Everyone commented on how good I looked. Then came the relapse/relax part. Before long and twice as fast as I had lost it, I regained weight from 75kg to 86kg.

I enrolled back into the gym and went on to another trending diet with meal replacements, measuring cups, spoons and scales. Nothing happened on the scale that mattered to me and my clothes remained unchanged for a whole year. Of course I did go from feeling clumsy and dreadful, regained a bit of glow in my skin because of regularly working out, grew a bit of endurance and actually made good fat-fighting comrades that made gym fun. This is around the time I met Rachel. I have known her around, and seen her at another gym at another time, but this is when we started the fat war together. And boy was she determined! She became an awesome motivation though I was not doing so great at being consistent and focusing. I had signed up for functional training boot camp. Going at it for one whole winter season, we were so resolute and intent to look thinner when summer rolled in that we braved the cold in early mornings to train on a car park ... OUTSIDE, NOT COVERED car parking area!

It lasted those three months, it became boring because of this and that, it wore out our system and then we ganged up for personal training. Fun and competitive, but it also fell on the wayside. Work took over. Kids took over. Life took over. This was between 2013 and 2014.

I slacked, she carried on until we reconnected again in 2016 at another new gym. She looked awesome. I grew envious as a toad. But gym was still WORK! And so distracting with a lot of the members looking fit and slim. And then she introduced me to IF. Intermittent Fasting, life has never been this awesome. I don't feel I'm on a diet or I can't eat. It is working beautifully, I can wear orange, yellow and pink ... and soon will be wearing all white comfortably loading!

IF has been a life saver, I mean I have tried a lot of weight-loss/fat-loss products: green coffee, ephedrine, two well-known diets that have created huge movements. I was taking some cheap little pills which I cannot even remember the name, Slim fast shakes/drinks, herbal life, flying elephant tea (where I did become a flying elephant because I was training and becoming fit but still packing mass!). Now I eat only one meal a day in most days of the week and twice during other days, without much effort or feeling like I have been given the slowest of death sentences. I can eat anything I want, and though knowing that, my body has somehow tuned itself to clean eating most of the time. And even though I started with minimal exercise, I have grown to enjoy jogging again, and have the drive and energy to train at least four times a week. I have a new-found body confidence and healthy outlook in life.

Intermittent Fasting Reviews

"So far I like the way it has cleared my skin. Strangely, I like the feeling when I am fasting since I normally feel an energy boost and feel lighter. I lost 7lbs after my first seven days."

M.H from USA

"I like being able to eat what I enjoy ... It basically means more 'me time' than eating more often. And it is surprisingly easy once you get into it. I also enjoy feeling hungry before my meals. IF makes my meals more satisfying and something I really look forward to. It makes me happy to know that I can do it any time I want to, or sometimes choose not to do it. I feel relieved knowing that I have a plan that is flexible and always works, whereas so many other plans require absolute adherence or else they simply will not work."

P.M from Canada

*"I have been doing 16:8 for about two years
and have lost the weight and kept it off since
then. I like the fact that I don't feel deprived and
I can eat some junk if it suits me. It is not a diet
but rather a lifestyle."*

G.G.V from Philadelphia

*"IF has worked for me because it has given
me discipline. That is what I like most about it.
Before IF, I would lose weight and gain it back
again. I had no control over food which I now
have. I have kept my excess weight off for
nearly three years."*

S.Z.B from USA

*"It is cheap! Not having to plan
a third meal saves me money."*

S.B from Auckland New Zealand

*"IF has given me the liberation and freedom
from being fat! I now have control over what
goes into my mouth and I am enjoying the
benefits derived from it."*

K.M from Botswana

*"I like that my life stopped being centered
on food. And when I do eat, I am fueling my
system instead of overloading it."*

S.B from USA

*"I like that it made me lose a significantly
larger amount of weight than I had
previously lost using various diets.
I love that it is easier than a diet."*

S.C from Italy

*"My favorite thing is that there is absolutely
no food that you must eliminate forever, as is
the case with other diets. I still drink, and I still
eat sweets, carbs and meat. However, I have
learnt by trial and error (and bad stomach pain
in the early months) that for the most part you
will find yourself eating healthier because you
don't want to be too harsh on your stomach. I
still treat myself to 'bad' food that I want, but I
don't overeat those things anymore because
quite honestly it makes me feel lousy when I
overindulge. IF really does help you to learn
about your body as to what works and what
doesn't. I lost 25lbs in three months."*

J.LR from USA

"I love the flexibility of moving around my fasting window to suit my ever-changing schedule. Most importantly, I love the health benefits that go hand in hand with fasting and the sustainability of this lifestyle."

C.G from Belgium

"I love that it is easy to follow."

L.S from Australia

"I do a combo of IF, Low Carb/Keto and weight training. I love the fact that I feel and look so much healthier, kind of like I have been reborn. At 52, I feel like a young lion."

C.B from England

"I like the feeling of knowing that I cannot eat from a certain time as it stops me opening the fridge at night. I have lots more energy than before since adopting to this way of eating. I find it easy to fast for a longer time. I have never lost weight on any diet until I adopted this lifestyle."

N.C from England

"I love how flexible and easy it is to stick to this lifestyle long term. It fits with my social life and I can alter my window to suit a coffee morning or a night out on weekends. I fast whilst on holiday too which means guilt-free enjoying food with everyone else in the evening! Additionally, there is no need to buy special food since there is nothing you cannot have. I make family meals for everyone which we all enjoy together. I eat carbs, sugar and fat with no calorie counting either! My body has really responded to this way of eating by shedding 13kg and it has been off for two years so far. I am looking forward to keeping it going long term."

M.F from UK

"I don't feel bloated all the time and even if my scales do not move as much as I want, I can still see the difference."

R.J from UK

"I think the greatest benefit of Intermittent Fasting is getting to know when you are really hungry and not hungry to avoid unnecessary eating."

N.P from Croatia

"IF stops me from just eating and eating without really being hungry. I am normally a grazer and IF has stopped me from doing that. I know I am getting health benefits and I actually listen to my body when it tells me that it is hungry since I have trained it to know my eating times. I came to realize that we don't need to constantly eat, we are designed to fast. Modern lifestyle has made us become greedy which pulls us from the basics.

I also love the way I don't feel like I am dieting and can take a day off for an occasion if I want to indulge without feeling guilty."

S.H from UK

"I do a combo of IF and Keto. My hair is thicker and skin so much better. I am 41 years old but I feel like I am in my early 30s."

R.Q from Malaysia

"What I love best is that I don't feel bloated anymore. I also notice that my energy levels have increased. It is not a diet it's a lifestyle change where I am losing weight easily and it is not complicated."

H.G from England

"I am 46 years old and have been doing IF for a year. Firstly to help with my health. Not eating after 6pm has helped me with indigestion issues. I love the control IF gives me. I have been doing 16:8 for twelve months and I enjoy many lovely, homemade, colorful dinners, and my husband has now joined me on this beautiful way of life."

L.R from UK

"I have been doing this for a month and I have lost a stone already. I am free from bloating without having to cook 'special' food just for myself. Since I have a teenage daughter, I want to avoid the 'I am on a diet' mentality in front of her. I am hardly hungry and feel I can encourage a healthy attitude to food with the 16:8 whilst not even drawing attention to it. There are disruptions ... just altering my times to eat has made a massive difference already."

C.T from UK

Do You Need To Connect With Others For Extra Support?

- Facebook: Just Eat – Intermittent Fasting Lifestyle
- Instagram: Just Eat – Intermittent Fasting Lifestyle
- Twitter: - @justeatandfast

Please share your thoughts and experiences with me at: www.rachelnekati.com

"Always remember that life is a marathon not a sprint, so pace yourself."

Acknowledgements

To My Dear Husband

This is a special dedication to my husband. To say that this man has been supportive would be an understatement. I remember the days when I was on my dieting roller coaster. He listened to all my latest weight -loss discoveries and patiently provided unconditional love and support without criticizing my latest crazy weight-loss intervention. When I think of some of the methods I tried, it makes me laugh. One that particularly comes to mind is the 'cling wrap weight loss'. This involved applying a special gel all over the body and then covering or wrapping my body with a special weight-loss cling wrap. And who was my regular wrapping assistant? Yes, my husband.

Throughout my weight-loss struggles he never judged me nor complained. Whenever I complained about my weight, he would remind me of how beautiful I am inside and out. As my gym buddy, we qualified together as indoor cycling instructors.

All in all, I am greatly thankful to him for all his support, acceptance and unconditional love. Thanks Honey.

To My Dear Daughter

Cheryl is not only my daughter, she is my adviser, supporter and my brainstorming friend. My daughter is my best friend. I remember one time recently when we were relaxing at home, I said to her, "Ms Chay, [as I call her] I want to write a book about my weight-loss journey."

She looked at me and said, "Mummy, if that's what you want to do, just write."

Well that is how the writing journey started. As my supporter and critic, I always ensured that I bounced my ideas off her. Cheryl always listened and assisted me throughout my journey. I am happy to say she also suggested this book's name, *Just Eat.*

We were on a family outing when I asked why she suggested that name and she said, "Every weight loss is associated with nothing but; don't eat chocolate, don't eat ice cream, don't eat carbohydrates, don't drink this, so for a change, with what I have seen you doing with your new lifestyle, you have been *Just Eating* and losing weight". Well Cheryl pointed out the fact that weight loss should be about the freedom to indulge in what you want and still lose weight. She also said that she has never seen me being less picky, less worried and less fussy about what I eat. She always sees me eating anything I want and then stop eating for a while and the fat melts away. Not only did she notice my body changing whilst enjoying pizza, pasta, ice cream, chocolate and bread with them, I was also less worried about being on any diet. Thanks my Princess.

To My Dear Son

Daryl is my breath of fresh air. He is the sun that always shines on me. One special attribute my son has is the ability to easily read my emotions and sometimes even my thoughts. He can easily notice when something is on my mind. After I told him about my book writing initiative he said, "Mum you should get ready to sell millions of copies". He is an optimistic, motivational and caring individual. He is my IT specialist. Thanks my Sunshine.

To All My Cheerleaders

I would also like to express my gratitude to my extended family and friends who assisted and supported me on my weight-loss journey as well as tasks associated with publishing this book. I am thankful for having such a supportive family and friends and most of them are already living the IF lifestyle. Thank you.

Rachel Nekati

References and Sources

(1) www.nytimes.com/2016/10/04/science/yoshinori-ohsumi-nobel-prize-medicine.html

(2) www.ncbi.nlm.nih.gov/pubmed/25540982

(3) www.ncbi.nlm.nih.gov/pubmed/25546413

(4) www.bertherring.com/ac/fast-5/fast-5-summary/

(5) https://www.scientificamerican.com/article/how-intermittent-fasting-might-help-you-live-longer-healthier-life/

(6) www.jneurosci.org/content/34/46/15139

(7) www.ncbi.nlm.nih.gov/pmc/articles/PMC4509734/

(8) www.marksdailyapple.com/fasting-brain-function/

(9) www.ncbi.nlm.nih.gov/pubmed/25546413

(10) www.ncbi.nlm.nih.gov/pmc/articles/PMC4257368/

(11) www.ncbi.nlm.nih.gov/pmc/articles/PMC3608686/

(12) marksdailyapple.com/fasting-exercise-workout-recovery

(13) www.ncbi.nlm.nih.gov/pmc/articles/PMC3106288/

(14) www.fatburningman.com/6-step-to-lose-fat-if-youre-over-40 problem

(15) spinalresearch.com.au/fasting-can-trigger-stem-cell-immune-regeneration/

(16) www.telegraph.co.uk/science/2016/03/12/fasting-for-three-days-can-regenerate-entire-immune-system-study

(17) leangains.com/the-leangains-guide/

(18) www.muscleandfitness.com/nutrition/gain-mass/become-modern-day-warrior-diet-broke-all-rules

(19) www.bertherring.com/ac/fast-5/fast-5-summary

(20) www.eatstopeat.org

(21) www.healthline.com/nutrition/the-5-2-diet-guide - section1

(22) www.nature.com/news/2008/080505/full/news.2008.800.html

Further Reading

- *AC: The Power of Appetite Correction* by Dr Bert Herrings (2015)
- *The Fast-5 Diet and the Fast 5 Lifestyle* by Dr Bert Herrings (2005)
- *Delay Don't Deny* by Gin Stephens (2017)
- *Feast Without Fear* by Gin Stephens (2017)
- *The Complete Guide to Fasting* by Jason Fung (2016)
- *The 8-Hour Diet* by David Zinczenko (2013)
- *The Obesity Code* by Jason Fung (2016)

Made in the USA
Middletown, DE
04 June 2019